I0825712

Quebec Covered Bridges

by Harold Stiver

Copyright Statement

Quebec Covered Bridges
A Guide for Photographers and Explorers

Version 1.0

ISBN #978-1-927835-39-5

Table of Contents

How to use this Book

For each of the 88 historical or Traditional Covered Bridges remaining in Quebec, we have included photographs as well as descriptive and statistical data. Traditional Covered Bridges are those that follow the building practices of the Nineteenth Century and the early part of the Twentieth Century or those built later that follow those methods. All of these bridges have had repairs done as portions wear out, and some may have been almost entirely replaced through the years. I have used "The National Society for the Preservation of Covered Bridges, Inc." list of what they consider as Traditional Bridges.

Following is data included for each bridge

Name: This is listed in bold type, and where there are other names, it is the common name or the name listed on an accompanying plaque.

Other Names: Underneath the Common Name in brackets, you will find other names that the bridge has been known by.

Nearest Region and Township are listed.

It is frustrating to go on an excursion to see something and not be able to find it. This book offers you multiple ways to ensure that doesn't happen.

GPS Position: This is our recommended method. Enter the coordinates in a good GPS unit and it should take you right there. You, of course, must use care that you are not led off road or on a dangerous route.

Detailed Driving Directions: Directions from a town near to the bridge.

Builder: If known, the name of the original builder(s) is listed.

Year Built: As well as the year built, if it has been moved it will shown with the year preceded by the letter M and, if a major repair has been done, the year will be shown preceded by the letter R.

Truss Type: The type for the particular bridge will be listed. If you are interested in more information on the various types of trusses, access "Truss Types" from the Table of Contents.

Dimensions: The length and number of spans

Notes: A place where you can find additional items of interest about the bridge.

World Index Number:
Covered bridges are assigned a number to keep track of them which consists of three numbers separated by hyphens.

The first number represents the number of the U.S. State in alphabetical order. Following number 50 for the 50th state are additional numbers for Canadian provinces. Thus the numbers 05 represents California.

The second set of numbers represents the Region of that state, again based on alphabetical order. Humboldt is the 12th Region alphabetically in California, and it is designated as 05-12.

Each bridge in that Region is given a number as it was discovered or built. Zane's Ranch was the fifth bridge discovered or built in the Region of Humboldt, California and it therefore has the designation of 05-12-05. Sometimes you will see the first set of numbers replaced by the abbreviation for the state, thus CA-12-05.

A bridge is sometimes substantially rebuilt or replaced and it then has the suffix #2 added to it.

Formerly Listed in County: Quebec used to list their covered bridges by county and this names the county for each bridge. The self-guided tours are listed by county.

Photographing Covered Bridges

Some standard positions
Portal: Taken to show the ends of bridge or bridge opening. This view, usually symmetrical, will include various signs posted. This is also a good way to get run over, so be careful!
3/4 view: Shows both the front and sides of the bridge, and is often the most attractive.
Side view: Taken from a bank or from the river, this gives not only a nice view of the bridge but usually allows for some interesting foreground elements.
Interior view: An image taken from the interior of the bridge will show some interesting structure but there is not a lot of available light. A tripod is important and HDR processing is helpful.
Landscape View: With the bridge smaller in the frame, you can introduce the habitat around it, particularly effective with colorful autumn foliage.

Using HDR(High Dynamic Range)
HDR is a process where multiple images of varying exposure are combined to make one image.

It has a bad name with some people because many HDR images are super-saturated, a kind of digital age version of an Elvis painted on velvet. However, the process is actually about getting a full range of exposure with no burnt out highlights or blocked shadows. This is an ideal processing solution for photographing Covered Bridges where you often have open light sky set against dark shadowed landscape and structure.

I use a series of three exposures at levels of -1 2/3, 0, +1 2/3, and this normally runs the full exposure range encountered. It is important to use a stable tripod.

One situation where you may need a larger series is shooting from within a bridge and using the window to frame an outside scene. The dynamic range is huge and you will need to have a series with a much larger range.

There are a number of software programs you can use to combine these images including newer editions of Photoshop. I use Photomatix which I have found very versatile and easy to use.

Best times for photographing bridges

Mornings and evenings are generally the best times for outdoor photography but the use of HDR processing makes it easier even in bright direct light. Although any season is good for bridge photography including the winter, fall foliage included in a scene can be spectacular.

A Short History of Covered Bridges

Let's deal with that often posed question; "Why were the bridges covered"

1. Crossing animals thought it was a barn and entered easily. I like this suggestion, it shows imagination. However, its not the answer although the original bridges normally had no windows and this is said to be because animals would not be spooked by the sight of the water.

2. To cover up the unsightly truss structure. I don't think those early pioneers were that sensitive, and personally, I like the look of the trusses.

3. To keep snow off the travelled portion. In fact the bridge owners often paid to have the insides "snowed" in order to facilitate sleighs.

4. It offered some privacy to courting couples, hence "kissing bridges". That is a nice romantic notion but no.

In fact, the bridge was covered for economic reasons. The truss system was where much of the bridge's cost was found, and if left open to the elements, it deteriorated and the bridge became unstable and unsafe. Covering it protected this valuable portion and the roof could be replaced as needed with inexpensive materials and unskilled labour. Without coverings, a bridge might only have a life span of a decade while one that was covered often lasted 75 years or more before repairs became necessary. Besides extending the longevity of a bridge, wooden covered bridges had the virtue that they could be constructed of local materials and there were many available workers skilled in working with wood.

The first known Covered Bridge in North America was built in 1804 by Theodore Burr. It was called the Waterford bridge and it spanned the Hudson River in New York.

For the rest of the century and into the 20th Century, Covered bridge building boomed as the country became populated and people needed to travel between communities. The cost of constructing and maintaining a bridge was normally borne by the nearby community and many bridges charged a toll as a method of offsetting these costs.

The period from 1825 to 1875 was the heyday of bridge building but near the end of that period iron bridges began to supplant them.

The number of Covered bridges may have numbered 10,000 but have now dropped to about 840 spread throughout North America. Many have Historical Designations which provides them protection and many communities are interested in protecting their local historical bridges.

Quebec Regional Map

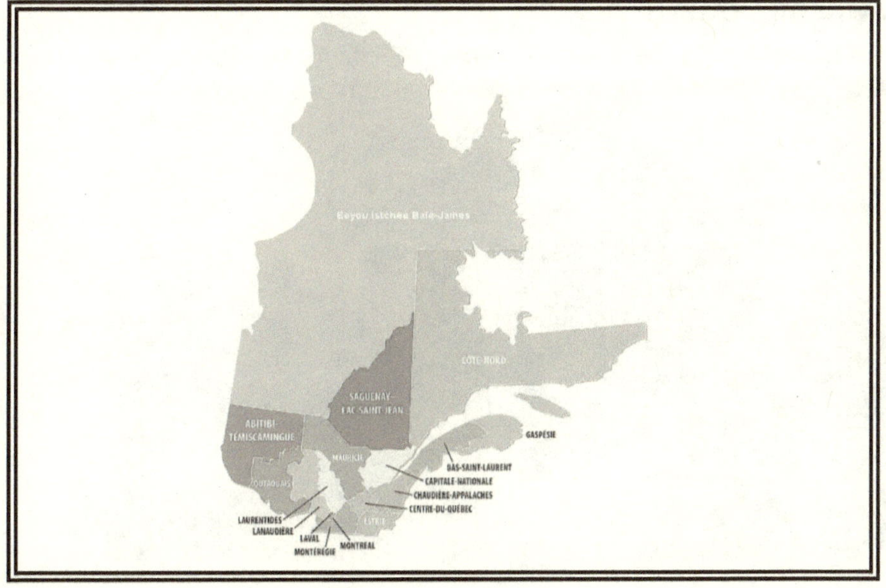

Pont Alphonse-Normandin
Region: Abitibi-Témiscamingue
Township: Béarn

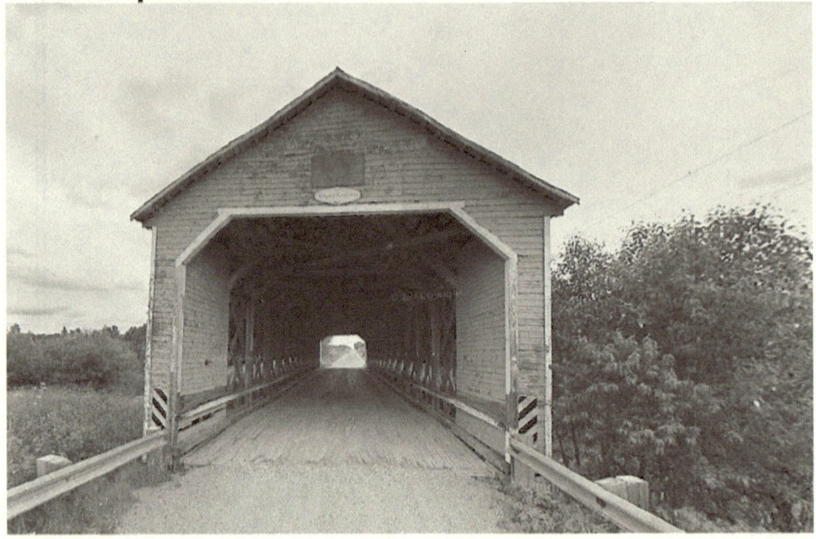

GPS Position: 48°44'04.0"N 78°09'49.0"W
Directions: From Saint-Dominique-du-Rosaire, head south on Rue Principale for 1.0 km and turn right on QC-109 S. After 2.5 km, turn right on Chem. Lavoie O and the bridge is 3.6 km
Crosses: Riviére Davy
Carries: Chem. Lavoie O
Builder: Ministry of Colonization
Year Built: 1950 (R2013)
Truss Type: Town variation
Dimensions: 1 Span, 40 meters (129 feet)
Notes: The bridge was originally built with arched portals but was changed to angled at some point. It was restored in 2013 when metal beams were added, increasing the load limit.

World Index Number: QC/61-01-05
Formerly Listed in County: Abiti-Est

Pont de l'Orignal
Region: Abitibi-Témiscamingue
Township: La Morandiére

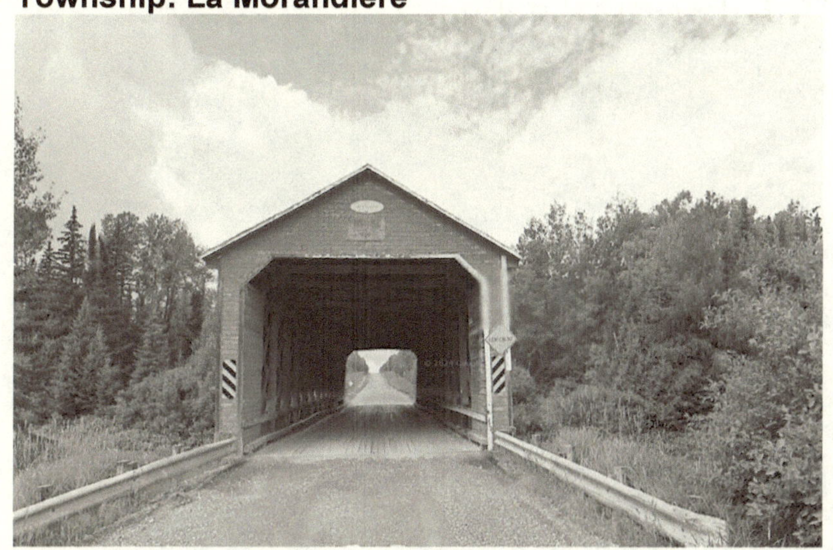

GPS Position: 48°42'17.0"N 77°33'14.0"W
Directions: From Rochebaucourt, head north on QC-397 N toward for 3.1 km and turn left onto QC-395 S where the bridge is 3.9 km
Crosses: Riviére Laflamme
Carries: QC-395 S
Builder: Ministry of Colonization
Year Built: 1942 (R2002)
Truss Type: Town variation
Dimensions: 1 Span, 37 meters, 118 feet
Notes: The portal was changed from an arch to angled in 2002. The work was done due to flood damage. In English, the name would be Moose Bridge.

World Index Number: QC/61-01-18
Formerly Listed in County: Abiti-Est

Pont Émery-Sicard

Region: Abitibi-Témiscamingue
Township: Dalquier - Duverny

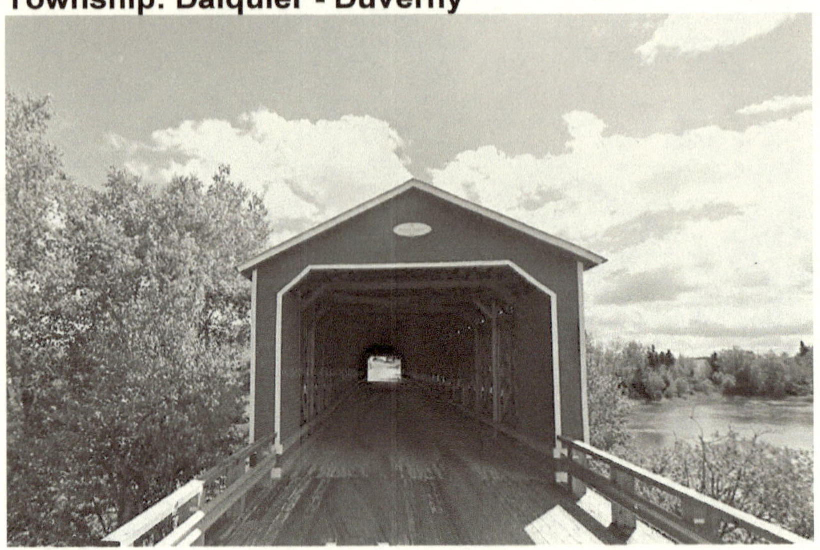

GPS Position: 48°38'36.0"N 78°00'18.0"W
Directions: From Saint-Maurice-de-Dalquier, head west on QC-395 S for 1.3 km and turn right onto CH Des 5 & 6 Rang to find the bridge
Crosses: Riviére Hurricana
Carries: CH Des 5 & 6 Rang
Builder: Ministry of Colonization
Year Built: 1946 (R1962)
Truss Type: Town variation
Dimensions: 1 Span, 66 meters, 217 feet
Notes: A substantial restoration was completed in 1962. The bridge is named for a local sawmill owner who also supplied the wood.

World Index Number: QC/61-01-22
Formerly Listed in County: Abiti-Est

Pont des Chutes

Region: Abitibi-Témiscamingue
Township: Rochebaucourt

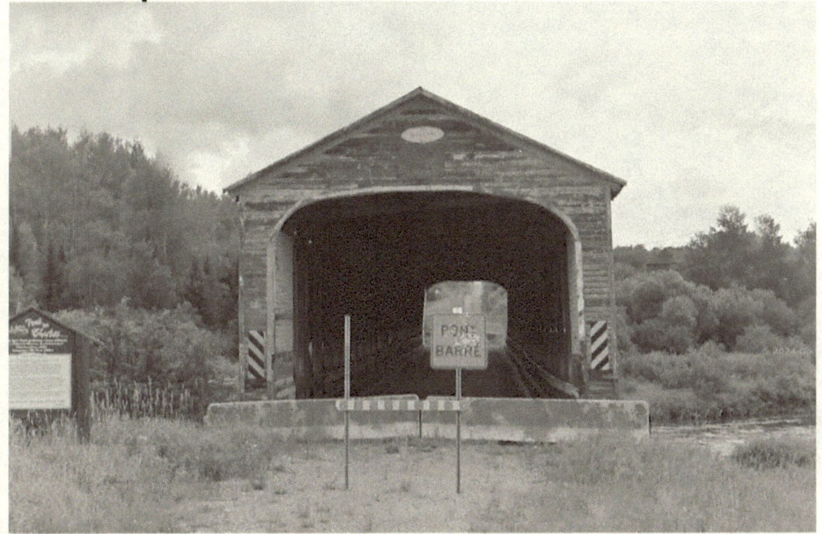

GPS Position: 48°42'17.0"N 77°26'41.0"W
Directions: From Rochebaucourt, head north on QC-397 N for 3.2 km and turn right onto Ch Des 7 & 8 Rang E. After 4.1 km you will find the bridge
Crosses: Riviére Laflamme
Carries: Ch Des 7 & 8 Rang E
Builder: Ministry of Colonization
Year Built: 1954 (R1961) (R1962)
Truss Type: Town variation
Dimensions: 2 Spans, 64 meters, 212 feet
Notes: In 1964 an abutment was washed away in a flood causing the bridge to break in two. It was repaired the same year. It was closed to traffic in 2010.

World Index Number: QC/61-01-25
Formerly Listed in County: Abiti-Est

Pont de l'Arche de Noé
Region: Abitibi-Témiscamingue
Township: Rochebaucourt

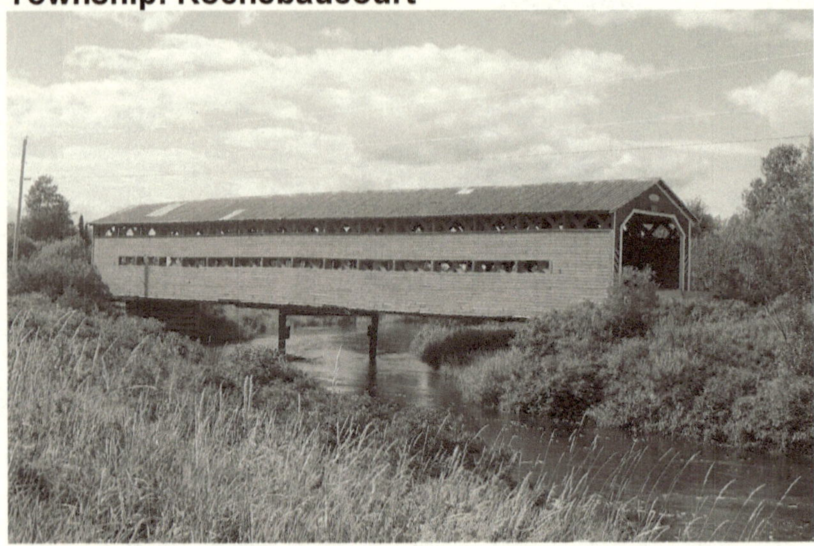

GPS Position: 48°38'46.0"N 77°39'03.0"W
Directions: From La Morandière, head north on QC-397 N for 3.1 km and turn left on 5e-et-6e Rang O, the bridge is 950 m
Crosses: Ruisseau Tourville
Carries: 5e-et-6e Rang O
Builder: Ministry of Colonization
Year Built: 1937 (R1985)
Truss Type: Town variation
Dimensions: 1 Span, 39 meters, 129 feet
Notes: In 1985, a steel support pier was added. It was painted red around that time as well. It was bypassed in 2010. The English translation is Noah's Arc as the bridge is said to float during a flood

World Index Number: QC/61-01-26
Formerly Listed in County: Abiti-Est

Pont Champagne (Vassan)

Region: Abitibi-Témiscamingue
Township: Vassan

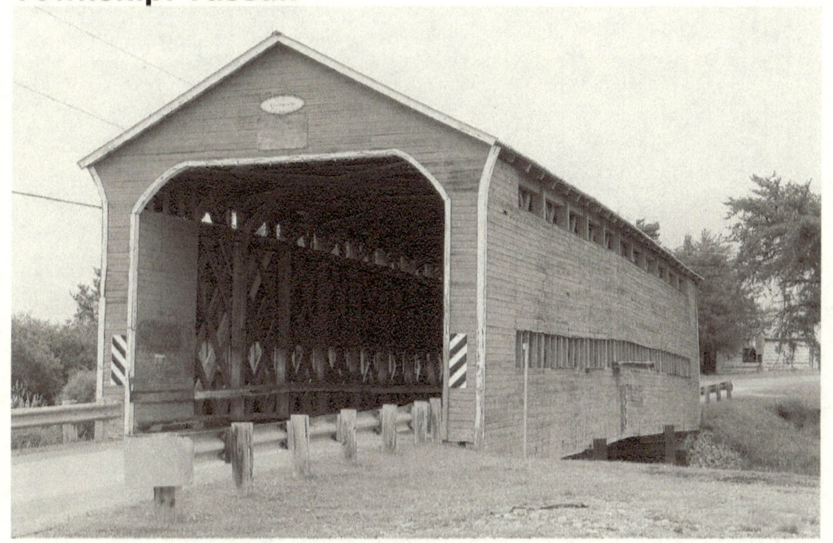

GPS Position: 48°12'53.0"N 77°55'32.0"W
Directions: From Crique-La Corne, head SW on Chem. de Vassan/QC-111 S for 5.3 km and turn right onto Rte du Chanoine-Richard. After 1.6 km, turn left onto Chem. du Pont-Champagne and the bridge
Crosses: Riviére Vassan
Carries: Chem. du Pont-Champagne
Builder: Ministry of Colonization
Year Built: 1941
Truss Type: Town variation
Dimensions: 1 Span, 32 meters, 105 feet
Notes: Formerly gray, it was painted red in the 1980s. In 1989 a metal support pillar was added. The maximum load was reduced to five tonnes in 2023 to protect the structure
World Index Number: QC/61-01-29
Formerly Listed in County: Abiti-Est

Pont Leclerc

Region: Abitibi-Témiscamingue
Township: La Sarre

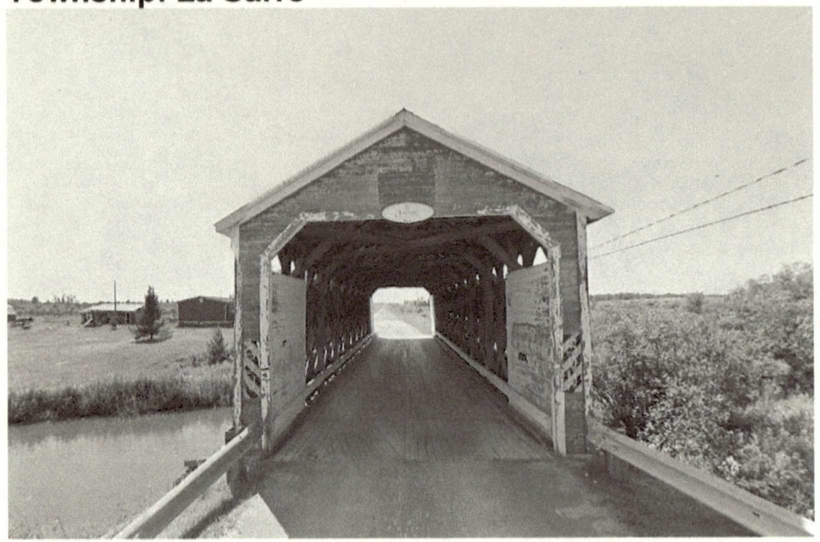

GPS Position: 48°50'11.0"N 79°16'33.0"W
Directions: From Bienvenu, head north on Chem. de la Calamité for 3.8 km. After Chem. de la Calamité turns left and becomes 8e-et-9e-Rang O/Rang 8 et 9 E, you will find the bridge in 2.1 km
Crosses: Ruisseau Bouchard
Carries: 8e-et-9e-Rang O
Builder: Ministry of Colonization
Year Built: 1927
Truss Type: Town variation
Dimensions: 1 Span, 25 meters, 81 feet
Notes: This bridge was built on a town truss variation. This design was modified by the Quebec Ministry of Colonization a

World Index Number: QC/61-02-05
Formerly Listed in County: Abiti-Est

Pont Molesworth

Region: Abitibi-Témiscamingue
Township: Macamic

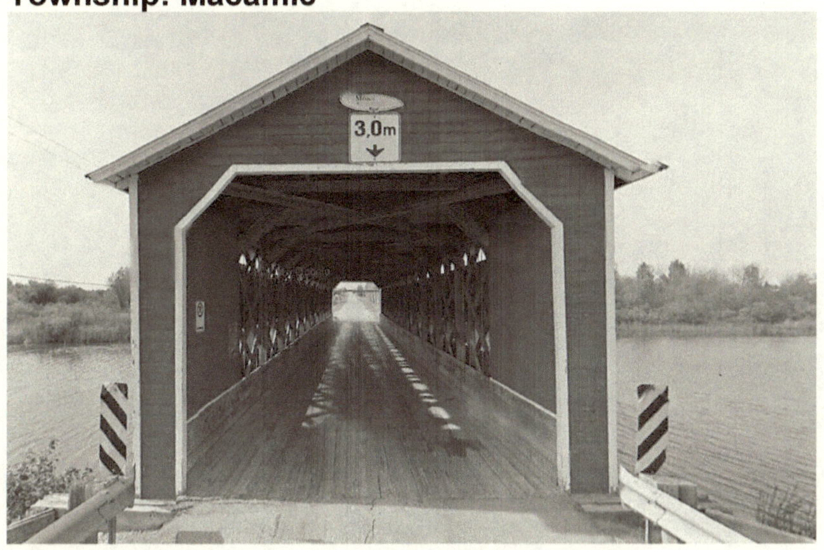

GPS Position: 48°44'56.0"N 78°59'39.0"W
Directions: From Macamic, head east on Av. 1e E/Rang 2e-et-3e O for 600 m and see the bridge
Crosses: Riviére Loïs
Carries: Av. 1e E/Rang 2e-et-3e O
Builder: Ministry of Colonization
Year Built: 1930 (R1950) (R1987) (R2017)
Truss Type: Town variation
Dimensions: 2 Spans, 35 meters, 113 feet

Notes: A central pillar was added in 1950 to increase its load capacity. Originally grey, it was repainted red during major renovations performed in 1987 and 2017

World Index Number: QC/61-02-13
Formerly Listed in County: Abiti-Est

Pont du Petit-Quatre
Region: Abitibi-Témiscamingue
Township: Des Méloizes

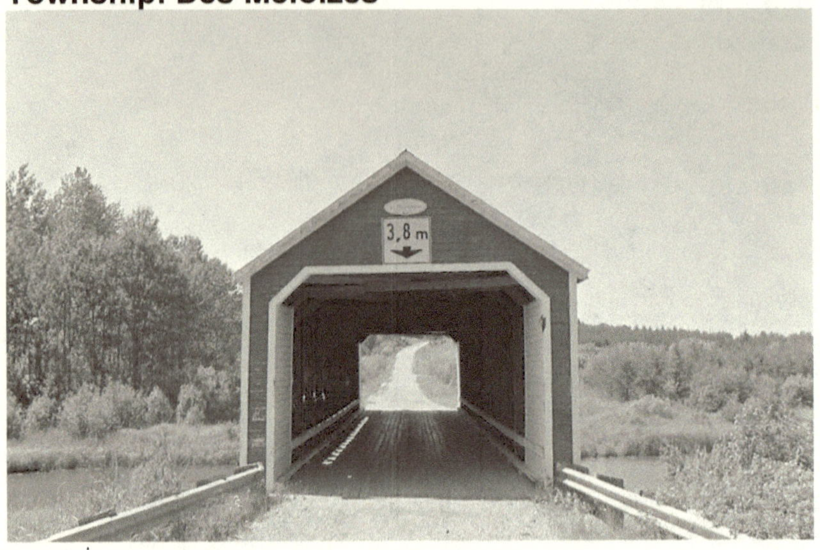

GPS Position: 48°54'29.0"N 79°19'35.0"W
Directions: From Abana, head south on QC-111 S for 4.8 km and turn left onto Chem. du Petit-Quatre, the bridge is 1.9 km
Crosses: Riviére Des Méloizes
Carries: Chem. du Petit-Quatre
Builder: Ministry of Colonization
Year Built: Ca.1950 (R1996) (R2012)
Truss Type: Town variation
Dimensions: 1 Span, 32 meters, 105 feet
Notes: This bridge had been beige and was painted red in 1996 and the portals were changed to angled. It was renovated in 2012, when the capacity was reduced to 5 tonnes from 12. Note the fine detail on the side windows

World Index Number: QC/61-02-20
Formerly Listed in County: Abiti-Est

Pont de l'Île
Region: Abitibi-Témiscamingue
Township: Roquemaure

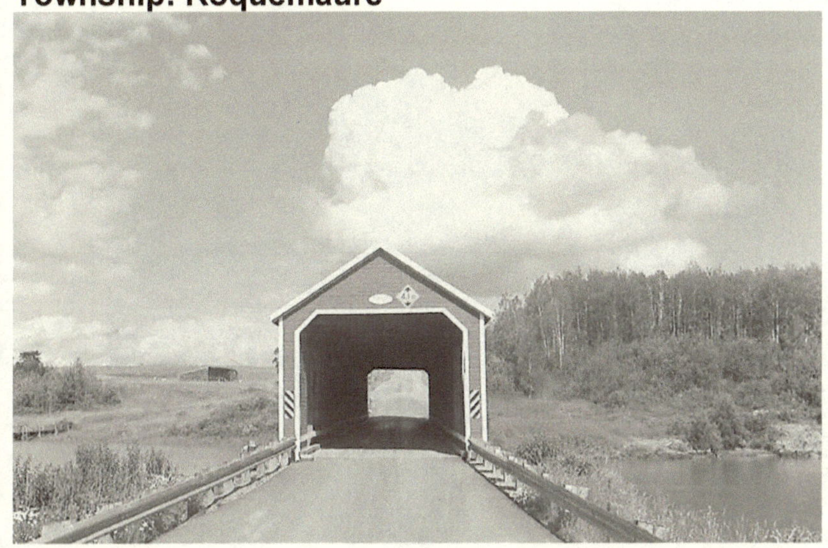

GPS Position: 48°41'30.0"N 79°24'27.0"W
Directions: From Clerval, head east on 2e-et-3e Rang for 10.7 km and turn right on Rte du 3e-au-4e-Rang. After 1.6 km continue onto Rte de l'Île-Nepawa for 7.4 km. Continue onto Chem. de l'Île-Nepawa for 3.4 km and the bridge is 950 m
Crosses: Arm of Lac Abitibi
Carries: Chem. de l'Île-Nepawa
Builder: Ministry of Colonization
Year Built: 1946 (R1997) (R2012)
Truss Type: Town variation
Dimensions: 2 Spans, 54 meters, 177 feet
Notes: In 1997, steel beams were added under the deck. The bridge underwent renovations in 2012. At that time, the colour was changed from beige to red.
World Index Number: QC/61-02-23
Formerly Listed in County: Abiti-Est

Pont Levasseur
Region: Abitibi-Témiscamingue
Township: Macamic

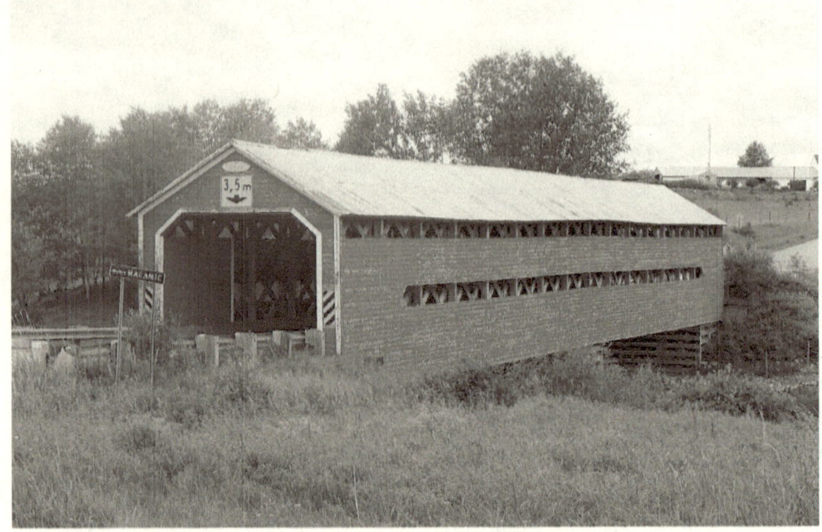

GPS Position: 48°50'07.0"N 78°53'22.0"W
Directions: From Authier-Nord, head south on Rue Principale/Rte Principale for 180 m and turn right onto Chem. du Pont-Couvert. The bridge is 2.1 km
Crosses: Riviére Macamic
Carries: Chem. du Pont-Couvert
Builder: Ministry of Colonization
Year Built: 1928 (R1946) (R1985) (R2015) (R2016)
Truss Type: Town variation
Dimensions: 2 Spans, 39 meters, 132 feet
Notes: A central pillar was added in 1946. In 1985 it was renovated. Following renovations in 2015, the load capacity was reduced to 8 tonnes from 12. It was repainted in 2016

World Index Number: QC/61-02-37
Formerly Listed in County: Abiti-Est

Pont Landry

Region: Abitibi-Témiscamingue
Township: Latulip-Gaboury

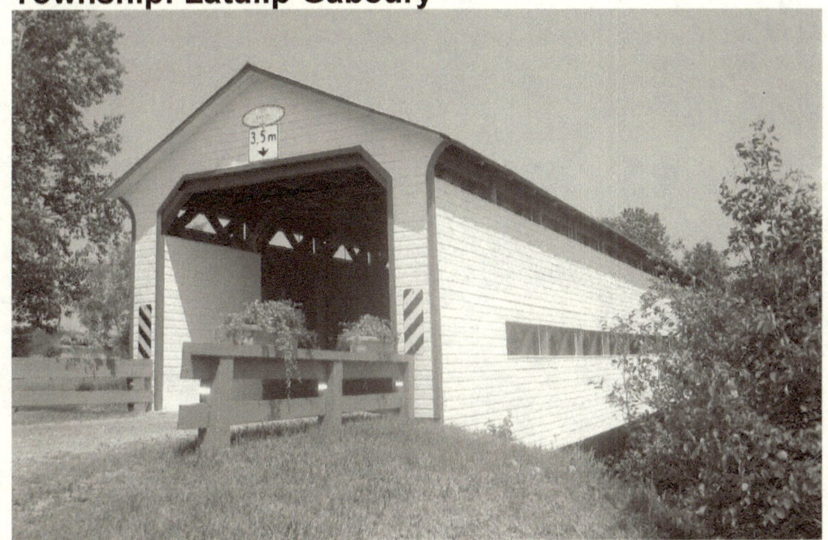

GPS Position: 47°23'49.0"N 79°02'50.0"W
Directions: From Latulipe, head south on Rue du Carr S for and continue onto Mnt du 9e Rang. After 2.9 km, turn right onto 9e Rang O and the bridge is 1.1 km
Crosses: Riviére Fraser
Carries: 9e Rang O
Builder: Ministry of Colonization
Year Built: 1932 (R1991)
Truss Type: Town variation
Dimensions: 1 Span, 33 meters, 107 feet

Notes: It was repaired in 1991 and repainted in 2010. In 2007 it was declared an historic monument by the local municipality

World Index Number: QC/61-70-02
Formerly Listed in County: Témiscamingue

Pont Dénommée

Region: Abitibi-Témiscamingue
Township: Guigues

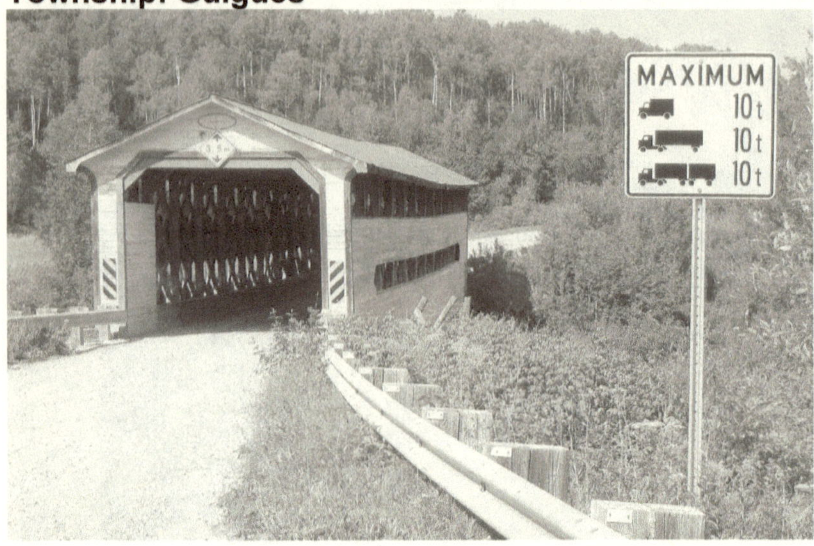

GPS Position: 47°29'05.0"N 79°24'26.0"W
Directions: From Kirwan, head north on QC-391 N for 2.4 km and turn left onto Rte à Tanguay. After 3.2 km, continue onto Rte du 6e-Rang and the bridge is 1.2 km
Crosses: Riviére à la Loutre
Carries: Rte du 6e-Rang
Builder: Ministry of Colonization
Year Built: 1933
Truss Type: Town variation
Dimensions: 1 Span, 29 meters, 97 feet
Notes: The bridge was lengthened by 10 meters in the 1950s, and was renovated in 1986. It is closed to traffic in the winter since 1975. The load capacity is 10 tonnes.

World Index Number: QC/61-70-04
Formerly Listed in County: Témiscamingue

Pont du College (Quelle Ouest)

Region: Bas-Saint-Laurent
Township: Ixworth

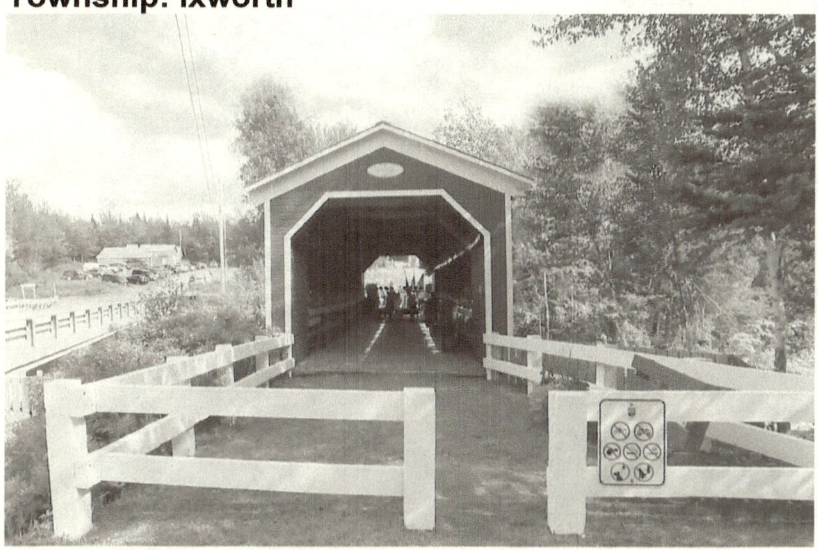

GPS Position: 47°17'33.0"N 69°57'06.0"W
Directions: From Saint-Onésime, head southeast on Rue de l'Église for 5.1 km and see the bridge
Crosses: Riviére Ouelle
Carries: Rue de l'Église
Builder: Not known
Year Built: 1920 (R2008) (R2017)
Truss Type: Town variation
Dimensions: 1 Span, 25 meters, 81 feet
Notes: The bridge was closed to vehicle traffic in 1978. The 2008 restoration was done using historical methods. The bridge was heavily damaged in February 2017 by a heavy snow load.

World Index Number: QC/61-32-02
Formerly Listed in County: Kamouraska

Pont de la Chute Neigette

Region: Bas-Saint-Laurent
Township: Neigette

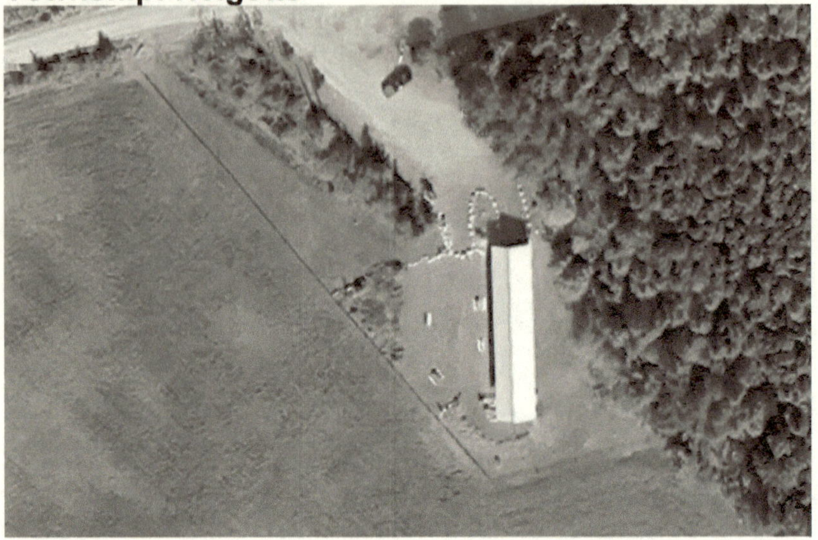

GPS Position: 48°27'05.0"N 68°18'53.0"W
Directions: From Neigette, head northeast on 5 Rang for 3.9 km and turn right to continue for 1.0 km. Turn left onto Ch Du Rang 2 Neigette E and the bridge is 400 m
Crosses: Riviére Neigette
Carries: Ch Du Rang 2 Neigette E
Builder: Not known
Year Built: 1933 (R2017) (M2017)
Truss Type: Town variation
Dimensions: 1 Span, 30 meters, 97 feet
Notes: The bridge is closed in the winter. It was moved to a field after being replaced by a modern bridge in 2017. In 2019, the Neigette Park was opened with picnic tables and parking.

World Index Number: QC/61-58-03
Formerly Listed in County: Rimouski

Pont des Draveurs

Region: Bas-Saint-Laurent
Township: Macpès

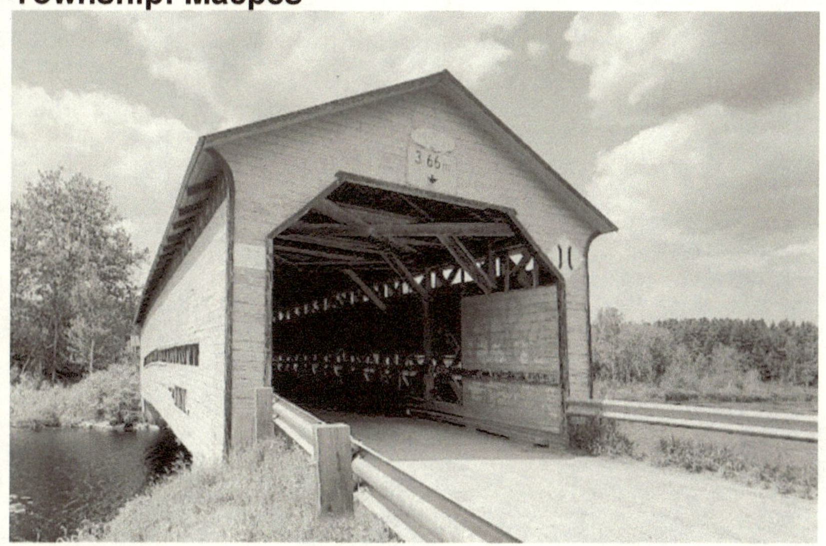

GPS Position: 48°21'50.0"N 68°22'07.0"W
Directions: From Neigette, head south on 1e Rang de Neigette O for 700 m and turn left onto Chem. du Rang-Double. Continue for 7.8 km and turn left onto Chem. du Pont Couvert/Rte du Pont Couvert and you find the bridge.
Crosses: Riviére Neigette
Carries: Rte du Pont Couvert
Builder: Not known
Year Built: 1930 (R1993) (R2000)
Truss Type: Town variation
Dimensions: 1 Span, 29 meters, 94 feet
Notes: The bridge is located in a tranquil country setting. The 1993 repairs were needed after the abutments collapsed in 1991. In 2000 maintenance work included painting.
World Index Number: QC/61-58-04
Formerly Listed in County: Rimouski

Pont Romain-Caron (Sainte-Jean de la Lande)

Region: Bas-Saint-Laurent
Township: Robinson

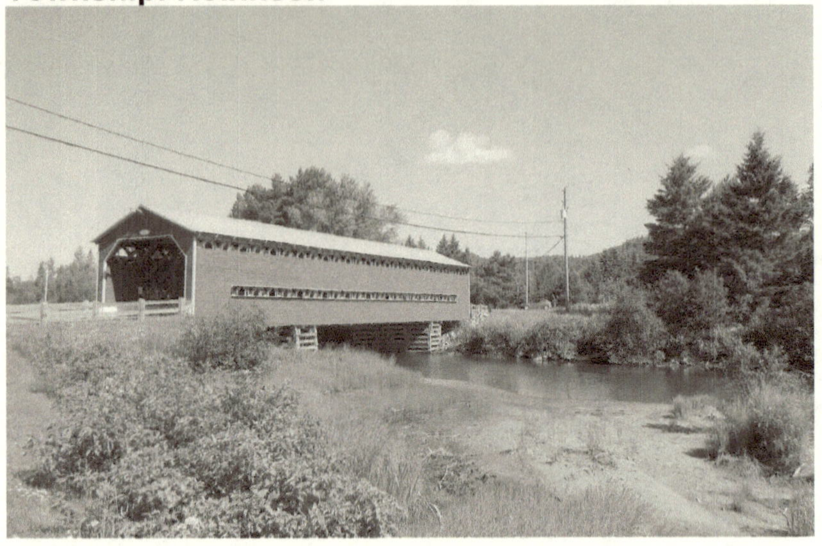

GPS Position: 47°23'43.0"N 68°43'13.0"W
Directions: From Lac-Thibeault, head south on Ch. Bellervie for 600 m and the bridge is on the right
Crosses: branche à Gerry
Carries: Ch. Bellervie
Builder: Romain Caron
Year Built: 1940
Truss Type: Town variation
Dimensions: 1 Span, 32 meters, 105 feet
Notes: It was bypassed in 1979 after the roof collapsed under a heavy snow load. A park was set up in the summer of 2013 which includes a sculpture and interpretation panels. The bridge is named for its builder.

World Index Number: QC/61-71-03
Formerly Listed in County: Témiscouata

Pont Balthazar
Region: Cantons de l'Est
Township: Farnham

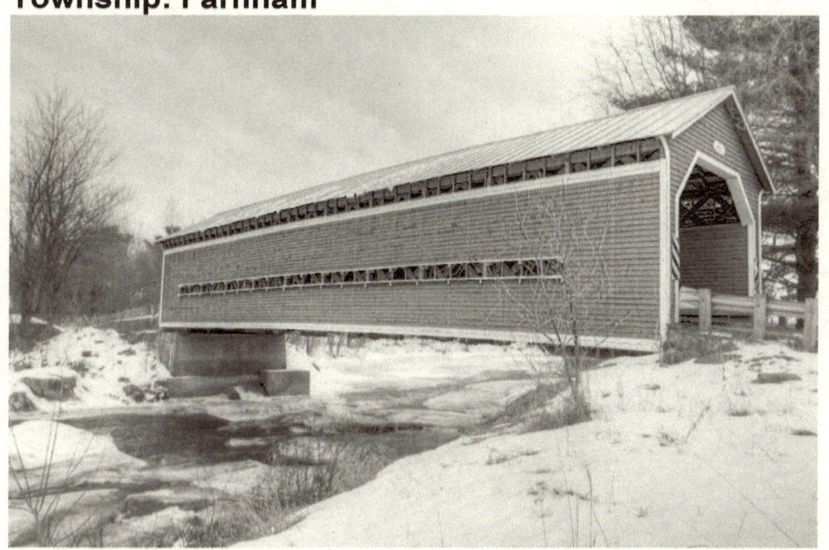

GPS Position: 45°16'51.0"N 72°50'07.0"W
Directions: From Adamsville, head west on Chem. Magenta E for 3.8 km and turn right onto Chem. Léger where you will see the bridge
Crosses: Riviére Yamaska
Carries: Chem. Léger
Builder: Not known
Year Built: 1932 (R2002)
Truss Type: Town variation
Dimensions: 1 Span, 27 meters, 88 feet
Notes: The bridge was named for Gustavus Balthazard, who lived in the area and who had approached authorities requesting a bridge be built. In 2002, the bridge was featured as an advertisement on Canada Savings Bonds.
World Index Number: QC/61-11-01
Formerly Listed in County: Brome

Pont Decelles

Region: Cantons de l'Est
Township: Farnham

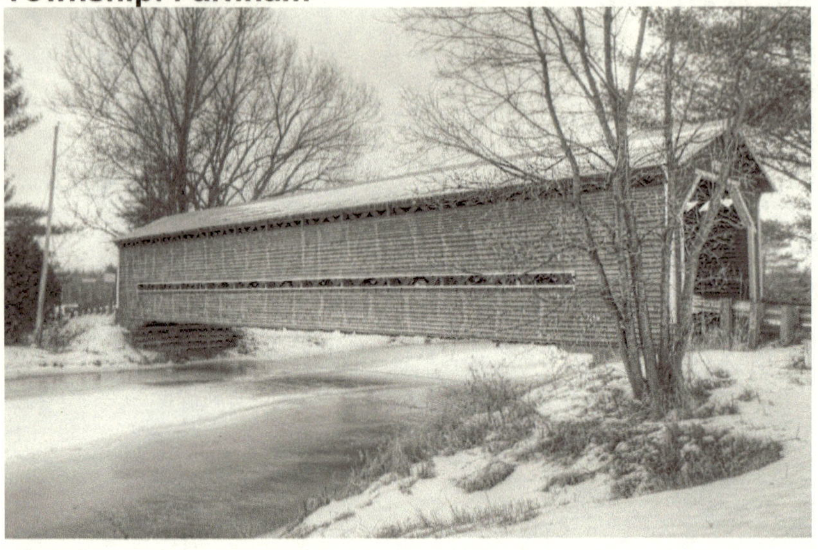

GPS Position: 45°16'51.0"N 72°45'43.0"W
Directions: From Adamsville, head east on Rue Choinière for 550 m and continue onto Chem. Choinière. After 1.2 km, turn left onto Chem. Fortin/Rue Fortin to find the bridge
Crosses: Riviére Yamaska
Carries: Chem. Fortin/Rue Fortin
Builder: Not known
Year Built: 1938 (R2007)
Truss Type: Town variation
Dimensions: 1 Span, 32 meters, 106 feet
Notes: Ernest Decelles presented a petition to authorities requesting a bridge and road be built to service the north side of Rivière Yamaska. The bridge was subsequently named after him. It was closed to traffic between 2000 and 2007
World Index Number: QC/61-11-02
Formerly Listed in County: Brome

Pont de la Frontière (Province Hill)
Region: Cantons de l'Est
Township: Potton

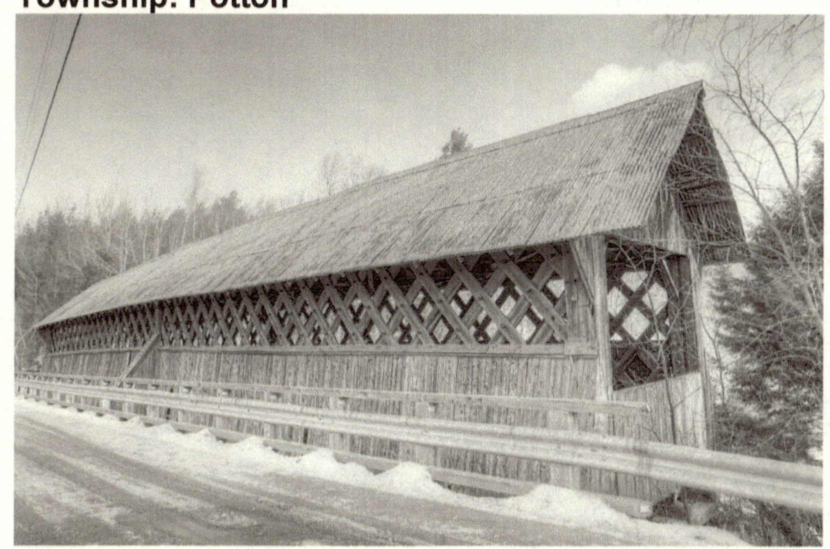

GPS Position: 45°00'42.0"N 72°22'25.0"W
Directions: From Province Hill, head southwest on Chem. de Province Hill for 2.0 km and turn left onto Chem. du Pont Couvert and the bridge
Crosses: Ruisseau Mud
Carries: Chem. du Pont Couvert
Builder: Not known
Year Built: 1896
Truss Type: Town
Dimensions: 1 Span, 31 meters, 102 feet
Notes: This road originally led to the U.S, border but is now closed. The bridge itself was bypassed in the 1960s. There is a picnic table on the deck,.

World Index Number: QC/61-11-03
Formerly Listed in County: Brome

Pont Drouin

Region: Cantons de l'Est
Township: Compton

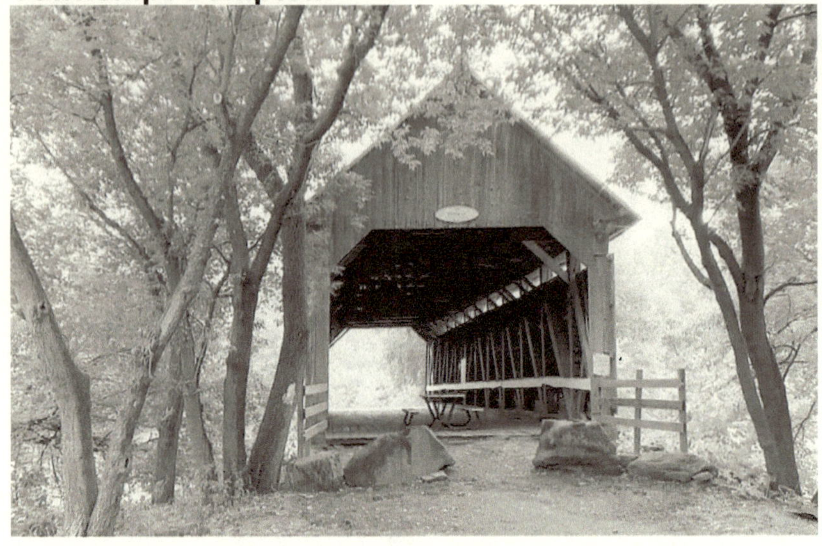

GPS Position: 45°15'50.0"N 71°51'05.0"W
Directions: From Waterville, head east on Rue Compton E for 800 m and continue onto Chem. Compton E. After 2.0 km, turn left onto Chem. Drouin and the bridge is 1.1 km
Crosses: Riviére Coaticook
Carries: Chem. Drouin
Builder: Not known
Year Built: 1886 (R1960)
Truss Type: Multiple kingpost
Dimensions: 1 Span, 30 meters, 98 feet
Notes: In 1960, it was reinforced by the addition of steel beams. The bridge was closed in the 1970s. In 1988 it was due to be demolished but was saved by local volunteers. The abutments were repaired in 2002.
World Index Number: QC/61-18-01
Formerly Listed in County: Compton

Pont d'Eustis

Region: Cantons de l'Est
Township: Compton

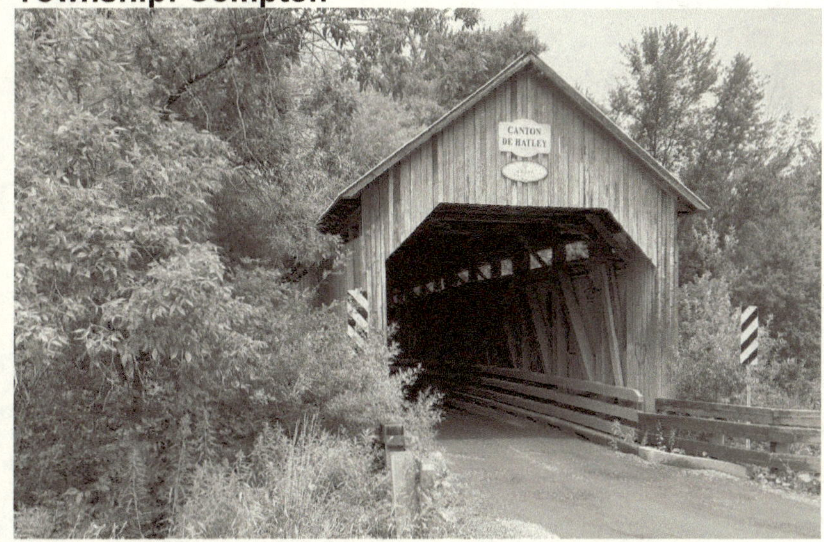

GPS Position: 45°18'11.0"N 71°54'48.0"W
Directions: From Eustis, head southeast on Rue Stafford for 800 m and you will see the bridge
Crosses: Riviére Massawippi
Carries: Rue Stafford
Builder: Hamlet Heavy Timberwork
Year Built: 2011
Truss Type: Multiple kingpost
Dimensions: 1 Span, 27 meters, 90 feet

Notes: The original bridge at this site was built in 1908. It was repaired in 1998 but began to sag in a few years. It was replaced in 2011

World Index Number: QC/61-18-02#2
Formerly Listed in County: Compton

Pont John-Cook

Region: Cantons de l'Est
Township: Eaton

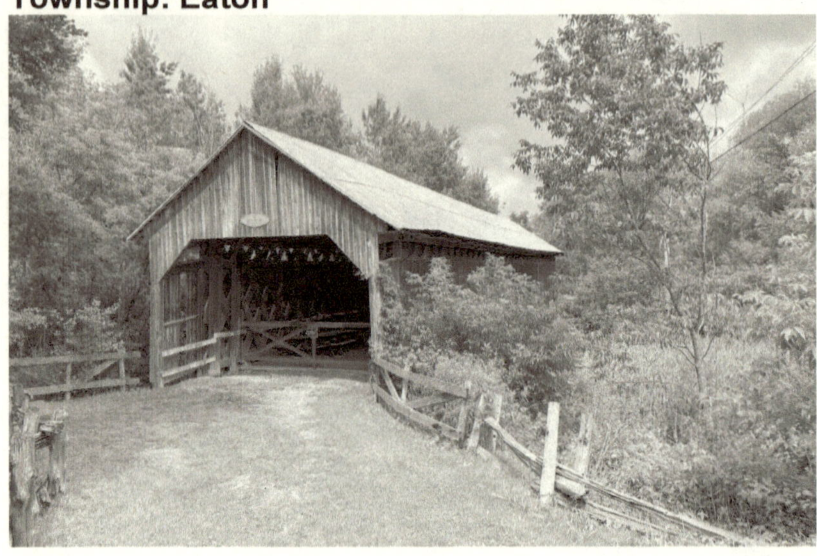

GPS Position: 45°25'19.0"N 71°37'57.0"W
Directions: From Cookshire-Eaton, head north on Rue Craig N/QC-253 N of Highway 103 for 1.0 km and see the bridge
Crosses: Riviére Eaton
Carries: Rue Craig N/QC-253 N
Builder: Not known
Year Built: 1868 (R2008) (R2015)
Truss Type: Town variation
Dimensions: 1 Span, 41 meters, 133 feet

Notes: The bridge is named for Captain John Cook (1770-1819), one of the first settlers in the area. The structure was closed in the 1970s and both portals were blocked in 2019.

World Index Number: QC/61-18-04
Formerly Listed in County: Compton

Pont McDermott

Region: Cantons de l'Est
Township: Eaton

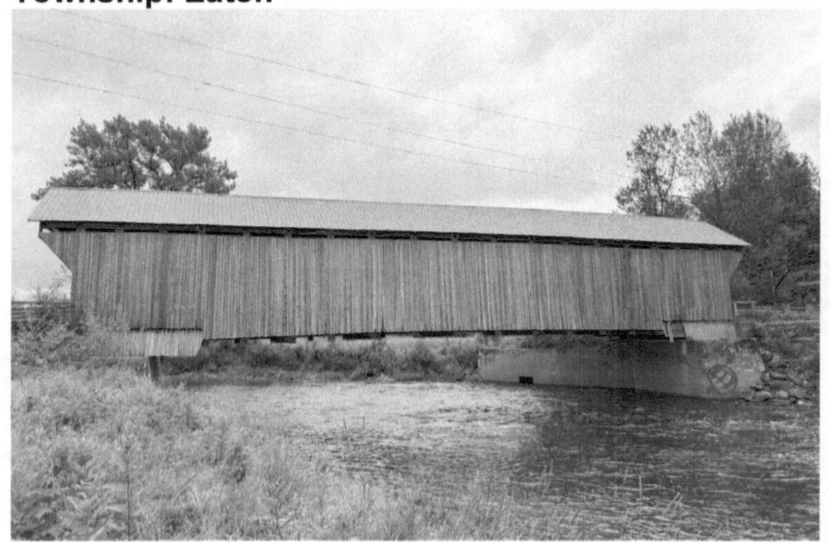

GPS Position: 45°23'34.0"N 71°33'22.0"W
Directions: From Lake's Mill, head southeast on Chem. Flanders for 2.2 km and turn left onto Chem. McDermott and the bridge is 1.3 km
Crosses: Rivière Eaton, North Branch
Carries: Chem. McDermott
Builder: Not known
Year Built: 1886 (R1989)
Truss Type: Multiple kingpost
Dimensions: 1 Span, 34 meters, 112 feet
Notes: In 1989 the deck and the bridge panel were rebuilt. The structure was closed in 2003, but reopened in 2008 after repairs were made

World Index Number: QC/61-18-06
Formerly Listed in County: Compton

Pont McVetty-McKenzie
Region: Cantons de l'Est
Township: Lingwick

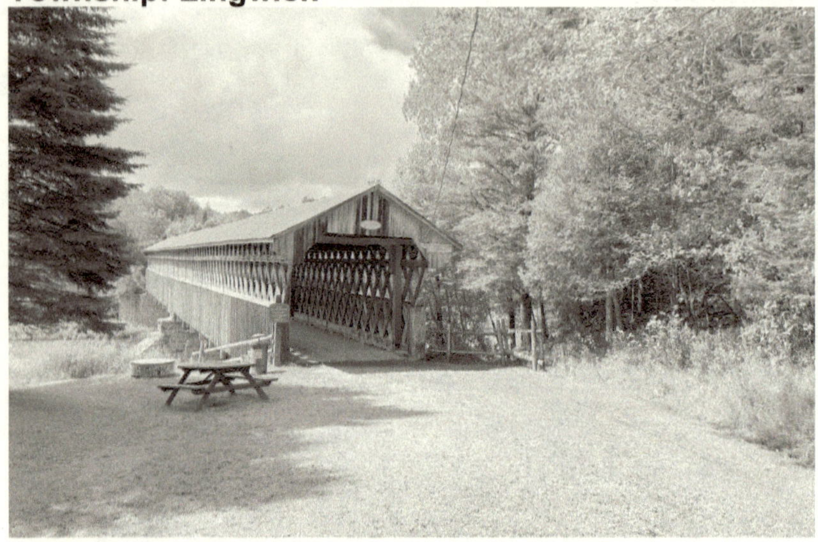

GPS Position: 45°37'10.0"N 71°23'42.0"W
Directions: From Gould, head north on QC-257 N and the bridge is 3.3 km
Crosses: Riviére au Saumon
Carries: QC-257 N
Builder: J. & J.A. McKenzie and William McVetty
Year Built: 1893 (R1950) (R2003)
Truss Type: Town
Dimensions: 2 Spans, 63 meters, 206 feet
Notes: In 1950, the shingle roof was blown off and was replaced by a corrugated steel roof. The bridge was closed in 1979. in 1991, the name was changed from Fisher Hill Bridge to the McVetty-Mcvetty Bridge in honour of its builders. The site has picnic tables, parking and toilets.
World Index Number: QC/61-18-08
Formerly Listed in County: Compton

Pont Guthrie (Pigeon Hill)

Region: Cantons de l'Est
Township: Seigneurie Saint-Amand

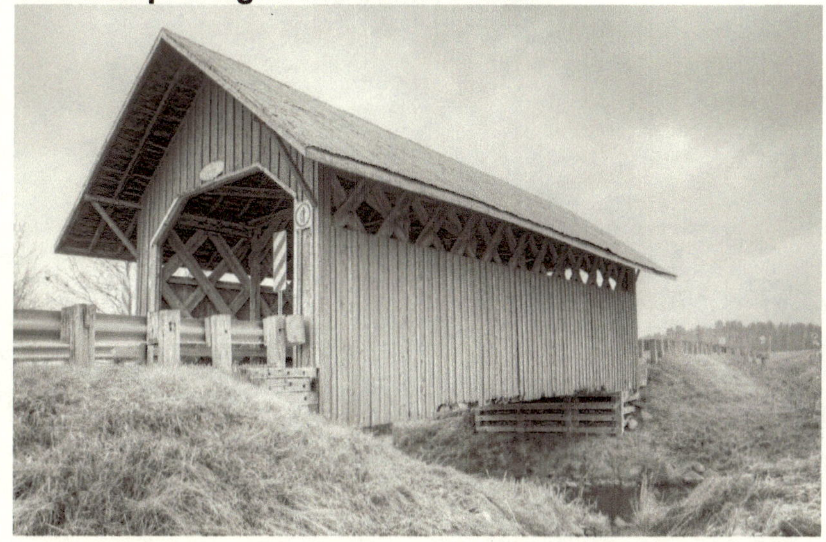

GPS Position: 45°03'56.0"N 72°57'29.0"W
Directions: From Campbell Corners, head north on Chem. Dalpé for 2.0 km and turn right onto Chem. Edoin where the bridge is 600 m
Crosses: Ruisseau Groat
Carries: Chem. Edoin
Builder: Not known
Year Built: CA. 1888 (R1993)
Truss Type: Town
Dimensions: 1 Span, 15 meters, 49 feet
Notes: At 49 feet, this is the shortest public covered bridge in Quebec. The structure was repaired in 1993. The bridge is named for a family that lived nearby

World Index Number: QC/61-45-01
Formerly Listed in County: Missisquoi

Pont de Freeport (Cowansville)
Region: Cantons de l'Est
Township: Dunham

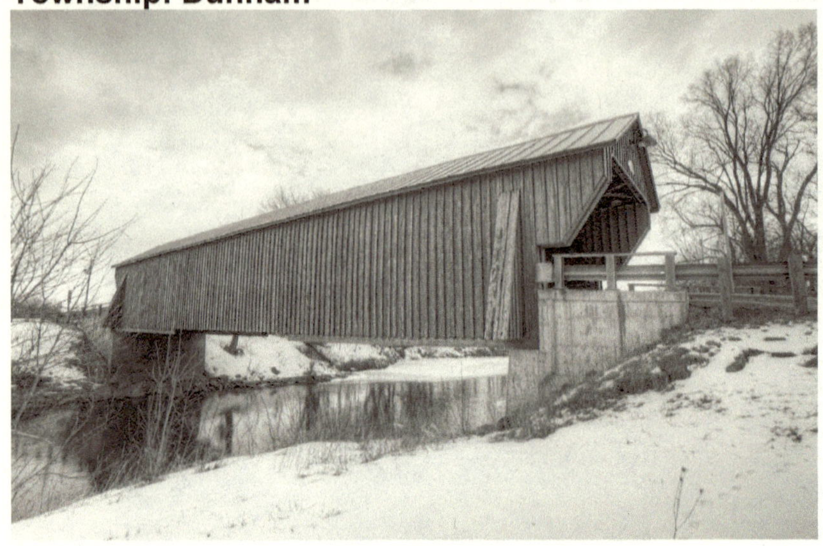

GPS Position: 45°13'06.0"N 72°46'02.0"W
Directions: From Cowansville, head northwest on Rue Albert toward for 2.4 km and turn left onto Rue Bell where you find the bridge in 350 m
Crosses: Southeast Yamaska River
Carries: Rue Bel
Builder: Not known
Year Built: 1870 (R2017) (R2020)
Truss Type: Town
Dimensions: 1 Span, 28 meters, 91 feet
Notes: The Bridge was heavily damaged by a truck in 2017 and again in 2020. It was named in honour of Freeman Eldridge, a builder of the area.

World Index Number: QC/61-45-02
Formerly Listed in County: Missisquoi

Pont des Rivières (Pike)

Region: Cantons de l'Est
Township: Stanbridge

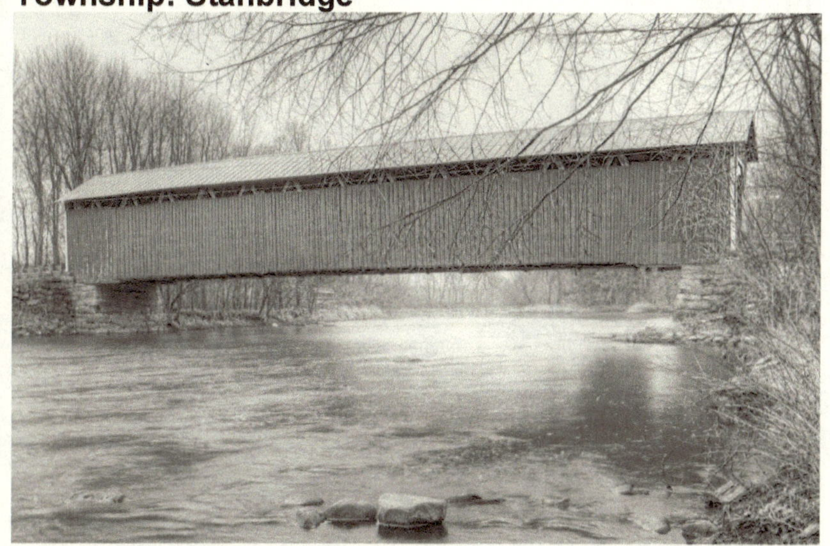

GPS Position: 45°09'28.0"N 73°03'04.0"W
Directions: From Malmaison, head northeast on Chem. des Rivières for 1.5 km and turn right onto Chem. Saint-Charles and the bridge
Crosses: Riviére aux Brochets
Carries: Chem. Saint-Charles
Builder: Joseph Reid and son
Year Built: 1884 (R1998)
Truss Type: Howe
Dimensions: 1 Span, 41 meters, 136 feet
Notes: The bridge is named after the brothers François-Guillaume and Henri Desrivières who built a sawmill and flour mill nearby. In 1998, the bridge was restored including the abutments, the roof and the flooring
World Index Number: QC/61-45-03
Formerly Listed in County: Missisquoi

Pont Cousineau (Bombardier)

Region: Cantons de l'Est
Township: Ely

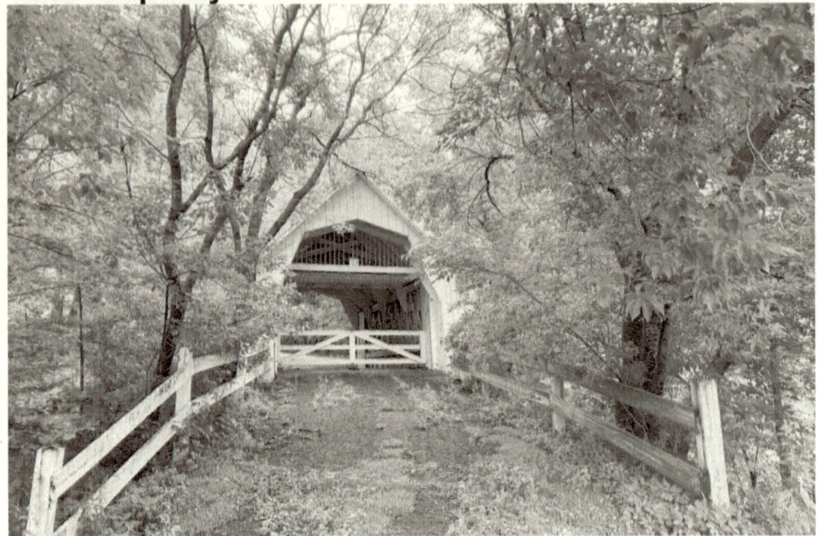

GPS Position: 45°29'54.0"N 72°18'50.0"W
Directions: From Valcourt, head north on Rue St Joseph for 500 m and turn right onto Rue du Moulin and the bridge
Crosses: Ruisseau Brandy
Carries: Rue du Moulin
Builder: Not known
Year Built: 1888
Truss Type: Town (R1960) (R1995)
Dimensions: 1 Span, 14 meters, 46 feet
Notes: The bridge is named for the Cousineau family who have owned the bridge since it was built. In 1960, reinforcement beams were added under the bridge. It was repainted in 1995. It is painted white inside and out.

World Index Number: QC/61-66-02
Formerly Listed in County: Shefford

Pont de Milby

Region: Cantons de l'Est
Township: Ascot

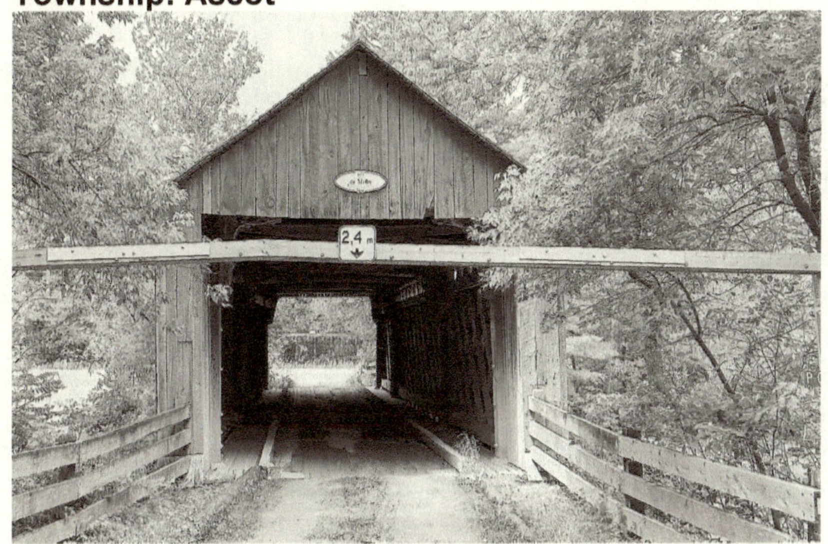

GPS Position: 45°18'54.0"N 71°49'23.0"W
Directions: From Milby, head north on QC-147 N for 200 m and turn right onto Chem. du Pont Couvert to find the bridge
Crosses: Riviére Moe
Carries: Chem. du Pont Couvert
Builder: Robert and John Hood
Year Built: 1873 (R1997) (R2007)
Truss Type: Town
Dimensions: 1 Span, 23 meters, 75 feet
Notes: In 1997, the roof and side panels were renewed. The bridge was closed to traffic in 2003 when it was found unsafe. In 2007, the bridge received a major restoration. The bridge was reopened seasonally in 2009. In 2023, it was changed to one-way traffic.
World Index Number: QC/61-67-03
Formerly Listed in County: Sherbrooke

Pont Rue Saint-Marc

Region: Cantons de l'Est
Township: Barnston

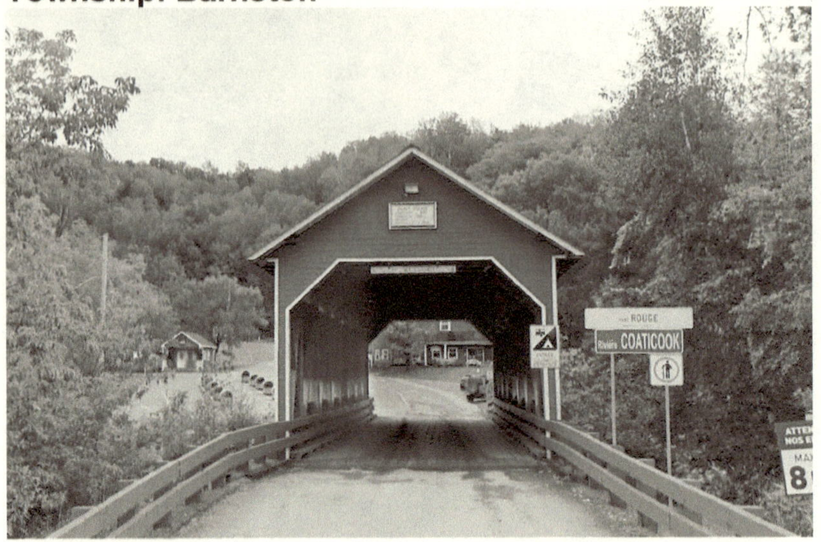

GPS Position: 45°08'43.8"N 71°47'54.2"W
Directions: From the town of Coaticook-Nord, head southeast on Rue Saint-Marc from Highway 147 and the bridge is 750 m
Crosses: Coaticook
Carries: Rue Saint-Marc
Builder: Technika
Year Built: 1998
Truss Type: Multiple kingpost
Dimensions: 1 Span, 18 meters, 61 feet
Notes: The original covered bridge at this site was built in 1887 and removed in 1979. The present bridge was built by Technika in 1998. The bridge is located at Parc de la Gorge in Coaticook.

World Index Number: QC/61-69-02#2
Formerly Listed in County: Stanstead

Pont Narrows
Region: Cantons de l'Est
Township: Stanstead

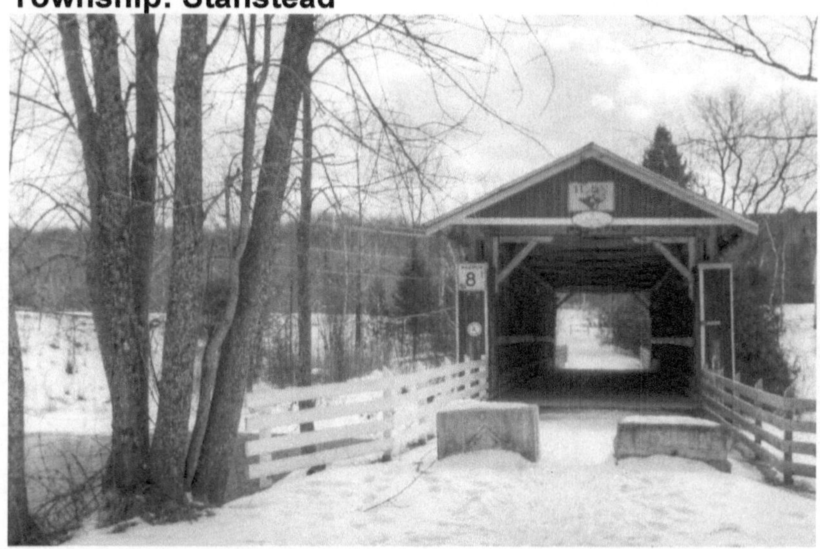

GPS Position: 45°05'32.0"N 72°12'03.0"W
Directions: From Applegrove, head northwest on Chem. Narrows for 1km and turn left onto Chem. d'Arrow Head. After 230 m make a left onto Chem. Ridgewood and the bridge
Crosses: Fitch Bay Narrows
Carries: Chem. Ridgewood
Builder: Charles and Alexander McPherson
Year Built: 1881
Truss Type: Town
Dimensions: 1 Span, 28 meters, 92 feet
Notes: The bridge was closed to traffic in 1977. Painted fences and flower boxes were added in 2015. The interior of the bridge was repainted in white in 2019 which hid some of the graffiti it has suffered.
World Index Number: QC/61-69-03
Formerly Listed in County: Stanstead

Pont Perreault

Region: Centre-du-Quebec
Township: Warwick

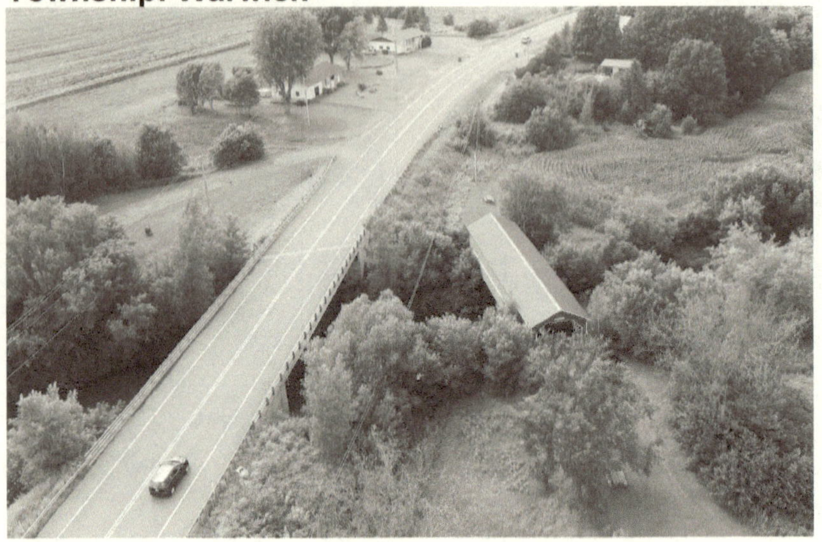

GPS Position: 46°10'57.5"N 70°43'00.1"W
Directions: From Notre-Dame-des-Pins, head west on 30e Rue from Highway 173 and the bridge is 650 m
Crosses: Riviére des Pins
Carries: 30e Rue
Builder: Not known
Year Built: 1929 (R2011)
Truss Type: Town variation
Dimensions: 1 Span, 29 meters, 97 feet

Notes: This bridge was closed to traffic in 1957. The structure was restored in 2011 by Construction Giron. The bridge honours Minister Joseph-Édouard-Perrault.

World Index Number: QC/61-04-06
Formerly Listed in County: Arthabaska

Pont Descormiers
Region: Centre-du-Quebec
Township: Tingwick

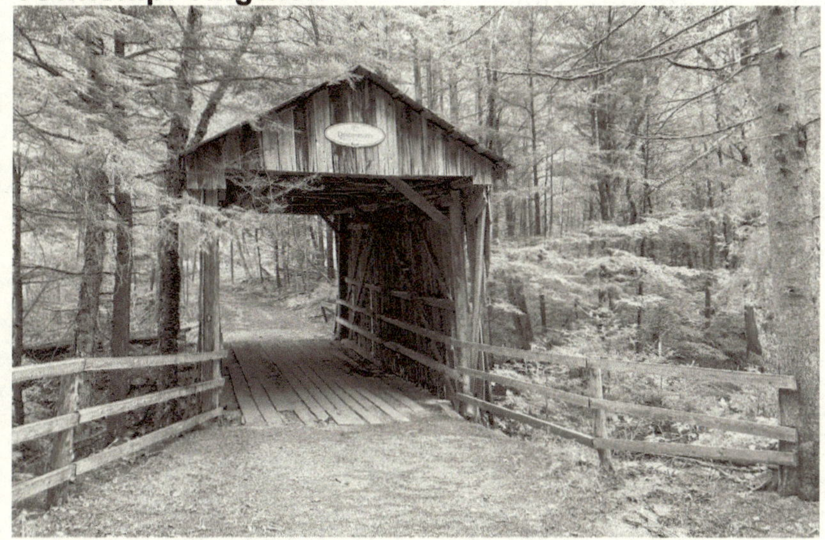

GPS Position: 45°53′51″N71°46′38″W
Directions: From Le Pont-Rouge, head southwest on Rang 10e et 11e/Rang Leclerc for 850 m and turn left on unnamed rd where the bridge is 700 m
Crosses: Ruisseau Laflamme
Carries: Unnamed road
Builder: Not known
Year Built: 1904 (R2011) (R2020)
Truss Type: Multiple Kingpost
Dimensions: 1 Span, 9 meters, 29 feet
Notes: The bridge is on private property. It received its name from former owners of the farm. The structure was restored in 2011 after it began to sink. New entrance ramps were added in 2020
World Index Number: QC/61-04-07
Formerly Listed in County: Arthabaska

Pont Davitt (Monaghan)
Region: Centre-du-Quebec
Township: Drummondville

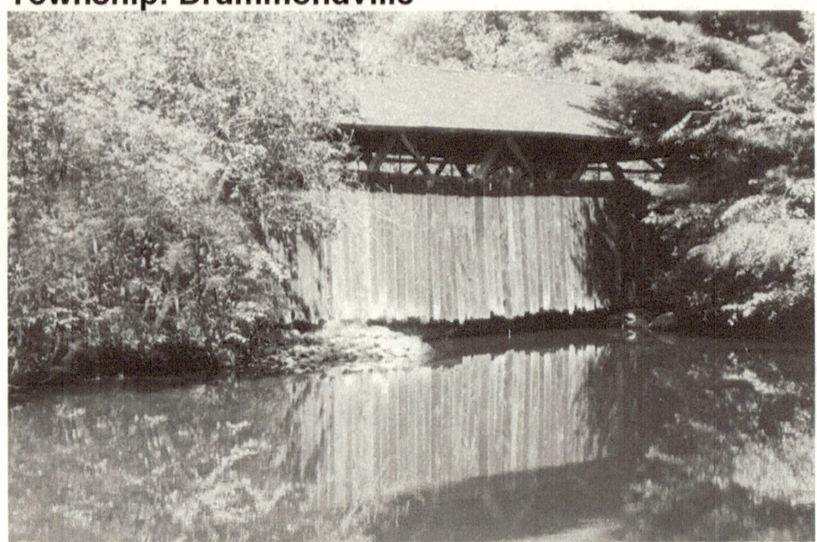

GPS Position: 45°53'37.2"N 72°29'18.6"W
Directions: 1370 Rue Montplaisir, Drummondville
Crosses: small creek
Carries: Rue Montplaisir
Builder: Not known
Year Built: 1878 (M1983)
Truss Type: Howe
Dimensions: 1 Span, 16 meters, 53 feet
Notes:This bridge was built in 1878 and located at Stanbridge East crossing the Rivière aux Brochets. It was disassembled in 1983 and reconstructed in Drummondville at the Village Québécois d'Antan. Each piece was numbered so it could be reconstructed . There is an admission charge.

World Index Number: QC/61-21-01
Formerly Listed in County: Drummond

Pont Paul-Émile-Giguère

Region: Centre-du-Quebec
Township: Durham

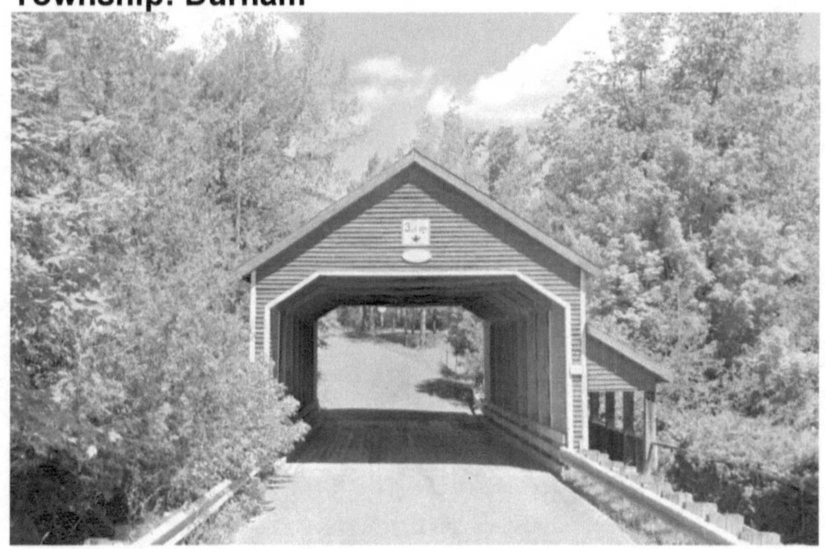

GPS Position: 45°41'26.8"N 72°16'11.6"W
Directions: From Richmond, follow QC-116 O to 9e Rang in Sainte-Christine for 11.6 km and continue on Rte Lisgar and Chem. Lisgar for 5.8 km where you will see the bridge
Crosses: Ulverton River
Carries: Chem. Lisgar
Builder: Not known
Year Built: 1994
Truss Type: Town
Dimensions: 1 Span, 22 meters, 72 feet
Notes: The original bridge was built in 1885 near the Ulverton Woolen Mill. It was demolished in the 1950s. The second bridge, built in 1992, burned down in 1993. The present bridge was built in 1994.
World Index Number: QC/61-21-05#3
Formerly Listed in County: Drummond

Pont Lambert

Region: Centre-du-Quebec
Township: Halifax

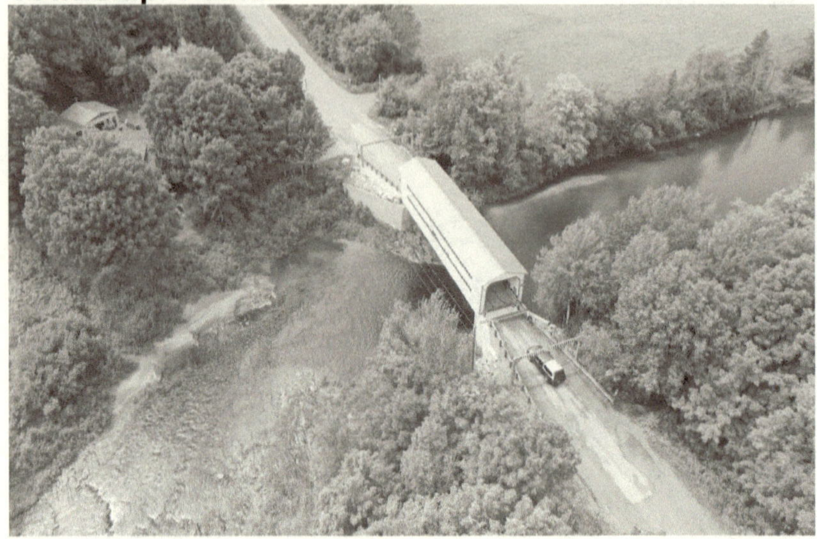

GPS Position: 46°07'41.0"N 71°45'55.0"W
Directions: From La Rochelle, head southeast on 2e Rang for 1.4 km and turn right onto Rte Lambert to see the bridge
Crosses: Riviére Bulstrode
Carries: Rte Lambert
Builder: Not known
Year Built: 1948 (M1925) (R2018) (R2020) (R2023)
Truss Type: Town variation
Dimensions: 1 Span, 27 meters, 89 feet

Notes: The bridge was originally called the Poirier bridge after a local family. In 1925, it was moved to its current location. In 2023 it was repainted white.

World Index Number: QC/61-44-08
Formerly Listed in County: Mégantic

Pont des Raymond

Region: Centre-du-Quebec

Township: Aston

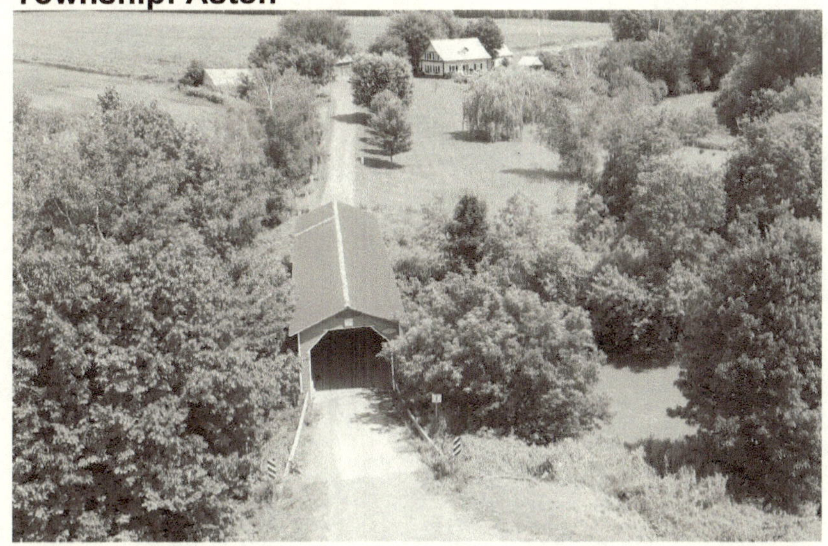

GPS Position: 46°15'36.0"N 72°24'08.0"W

Directions: From Saint-Célestin-Station, head north on Rang Saint-Michel for 3.8 km and turn left onto Rte de la Seine and the bridge is 1.8 km

Crosses: Rivière Saint-Wenceslas (Blanche)

Carries: Rte de la Seine

Builder: Not known

Year Built: 1928

Truss Type: Town variation

Dimensions: 1 Span, 30 meters, 97 feet

Notes: Arson attacks were made on the structure twice in 2000. It is closed in the winter although still easy to see. It has a load capacity of 12 tonnes

World Index Number: QC/61-51-01

Formerly Listed in County: Nicolet

Pont-Etienne Poirier (Sainte-Cèlestine)

Region: Centre-du-Quebec
Township: Aston

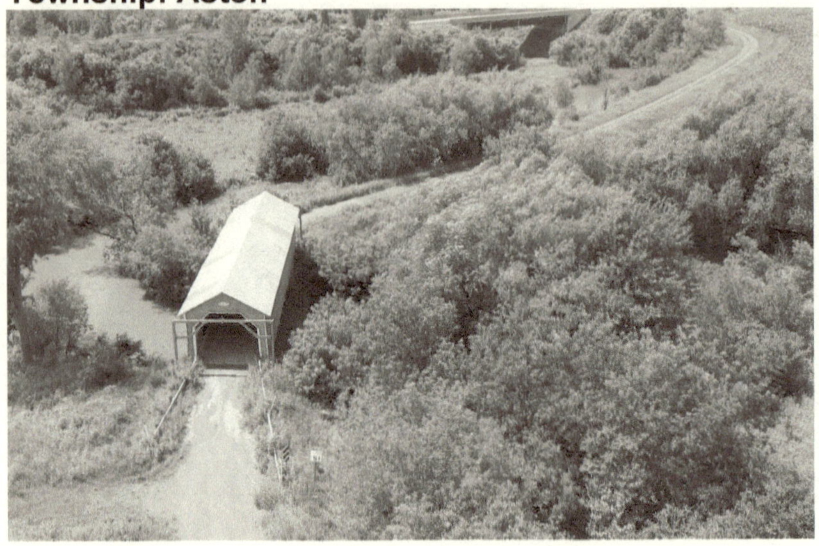

GPS Position: 46°11'50.0"N 72°23'24.0"W
Directions: From Saint-Célestin, head northeast on QC-226 E for 1.7 km and continue onto Anc. Rte 161. In 3.9 km turn right onto Rang Pellerin and the bridge is 1.0 km
Crosses: Rivière Saint-Wenceslas (Blanche)
Carries: Rang Pellerin
Builder: Not known
Year Built: 1905
Truss Type: Town variation
Dimensions: 1 Span, 25 meters, 81 feet
Notes: The road is closed in the winter but the bridge is easy to visit. Height restrictors were installed in 1991. The bridge is named for a local pioneer from the area

World Index Number: QC/61-51-03
Formerly Listed in County: Nicolet

Pont de Saint-Placide-de-Charlevoix

Region: Charlevoix
Township: Seigneurie Beaupré

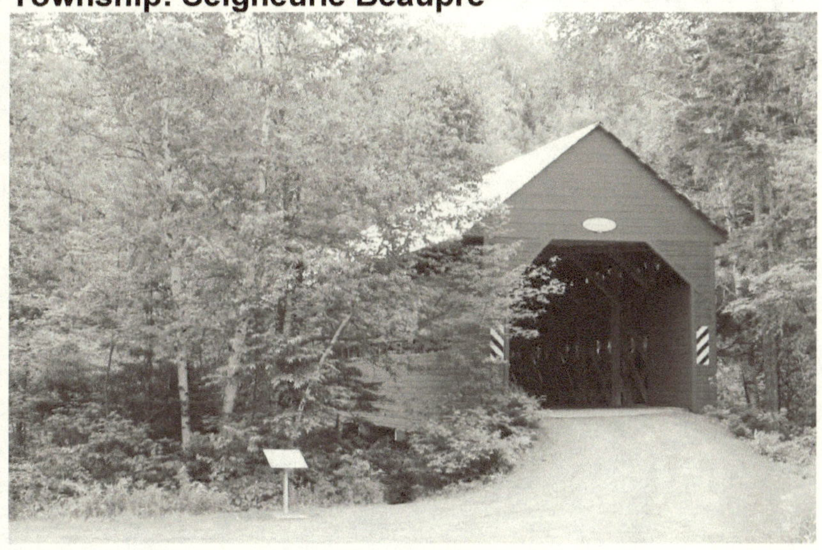

GPS Position: 47°24'28.0"N 70°37'03.0"W
Directions: From Saint-Placide-de-Charlevoix, head southwest on Rang St Placide S for 60 m and turn left onto Chem. du Pont Couvert and the bridge is 700 m
Crosses: Rivière Bras du Nord-Ouest
Carries: Chem. du Pont Couvert
Builder: Joseph Normandeau
Year Built: 1926 (R1995) (R2023)
Truss Type: Town variation
Dimensions: 1 Span, 34 meters, 113 feet
Notes: The road was previously closed in winter but is now open after improvements. The load capacity was changed to 5 tonnes from 12 in 2012. The roof was replaced in 2023 after damage by snow load.
World Index Number: QC/61-14-03
Formerly Listed in County: Charlevoix

Pont Perrault

Region: Chaudière-Appalaches
Township: Seigneurie Rigaud/Vaudreuil

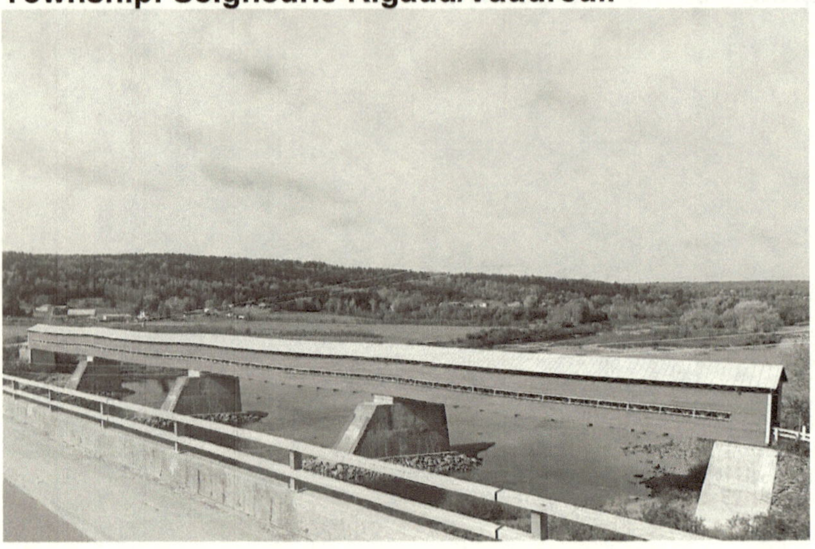

GPS Position: 45°57'23.0"N 72°00'24.0"W
Directions: From Warwick, head northwest on Rte St Albert for 1.0 km and the bridge
Crosses: Rivière Chaudière
Carries: Rte St Albert
Builder: Not known
Year Built: 1928 (R2022)
Truss Type: Town variation
Dimensions: 4 Span, 150 meters, 495 feet
Notes: At 495 feet, the bridge is the second longest covered bridge in Quebec. The bridge was closed to vehicle traffic in 1969. After the 2022 restoration, the bridge was opened to pedestrian and cycle traffic

World Index Number: QC/61-06-01
Formerly Listed in County: Beauce

Pont Bolduc
Region: Chaudière-Appalaches
Township: Tring

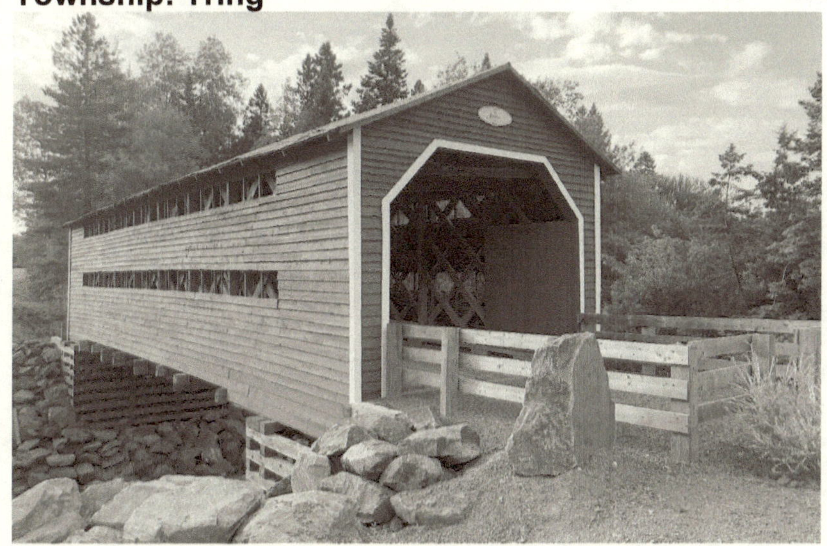

GPS Position: 46°07'43.0"N 70°59'15.0"W
Directions: From Sainte-Clotilde-de-Beauce, head northeast on Rte du Moulin for 2.7 km and turn right onto 7e Rang/Rang 7e N where the bridge is 2.0 km
Crosses: Rivière Fortin-Dupuis
Carries: 7e Rang/Rang 7e N
Builder: Lucien Bolduc
Year Built: 1937 (M1942)
Truss Type: Town variation
Dimensions: 1Span, 21 meters, 73 feet
Notes: In 2012 it was decided to move the bridge 13 meters to build a modern bridge in its place. The structure was moved from its abutments to a field and in 2014 it was replaced on the new ones. There is parking and picnic tables provided.
World Index Number: QC/61-06-02
Formerly Listed in County: Beauce

Pont Napoléon-Grondin
Region: Chaudière-Appalaches
Township: Schenley

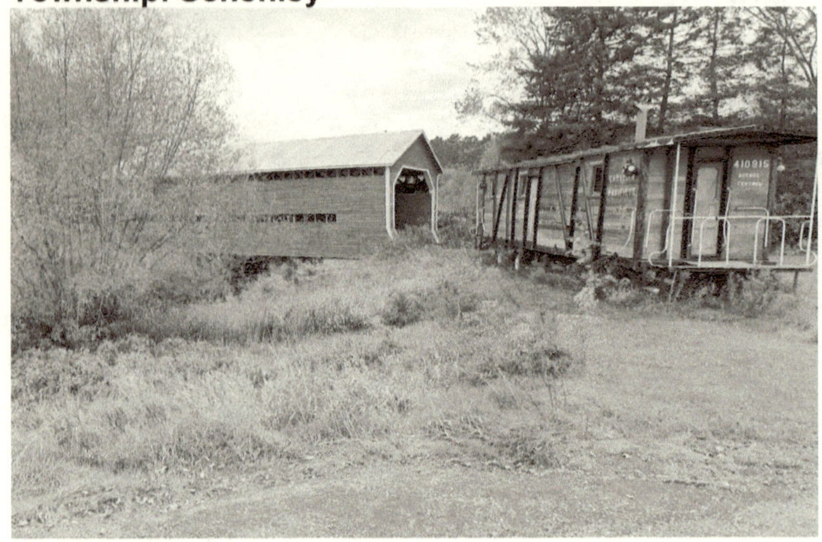

GPS Position: 46°03'31.7"N 70°54'29.2"W
Directions: From Saint-Éphrem-de-Beauce, head northeast on QC-271 S for 4.3 km ,and you will find the bridge
Crosses: small brook
Carries: QC-271 S
Builder: Not known
Year Built: 1933 (M1992) (R1993)
Truss Type: Town variation
Dimensions: 1 Span, 20 meters, 65 feet

Notes: The bridge was damaged by a storm in 1992 and a few days later. Pierre Mathieu moved the structure to private property and then reconstructed a shorter version.

World Index Number: QC/61-06-06
Formerly Listed in County: Beauce

Pont du Sault

Region: Chaudière-Appalaches
Township: Casgrain

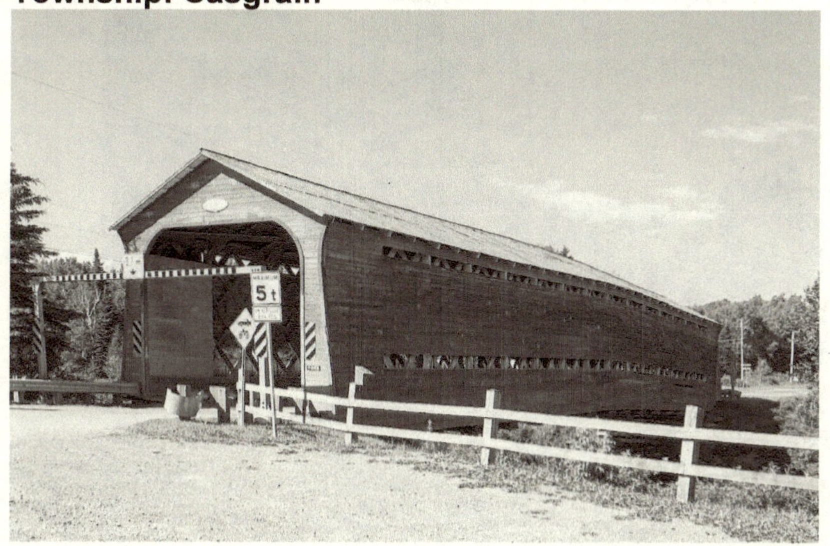

GPS Position: 46°55'08.0"N 69°53'46.0"W
Directions: From Saint-Pamphile, head southwest on QC-204 O for 9.4 km and turn right onto Rte du Sault. After 3.3 km turn right onto 4e Rang E and the bridge
Crosses: Grande Rivière Noir
Carries: 4e Rang E
Builder: Not known
Year Built: 1943 (R1990) (R1998)
Truss Type: Town variation
Dimensions: 1 Span, 39 meters, 129 feet
Notes: Major repairs were made in 1990. This included painting the panelling grey with red mouldings. The panelling had formerly been yellow. The approaches were repaired in 1998.
World Index Number: QC/61-39-01
Formerly Listed in County: L'Islet

Pont Saint-André

Region: Chaudière-Appalaches
Township: Seigneurie Saint-Gilles

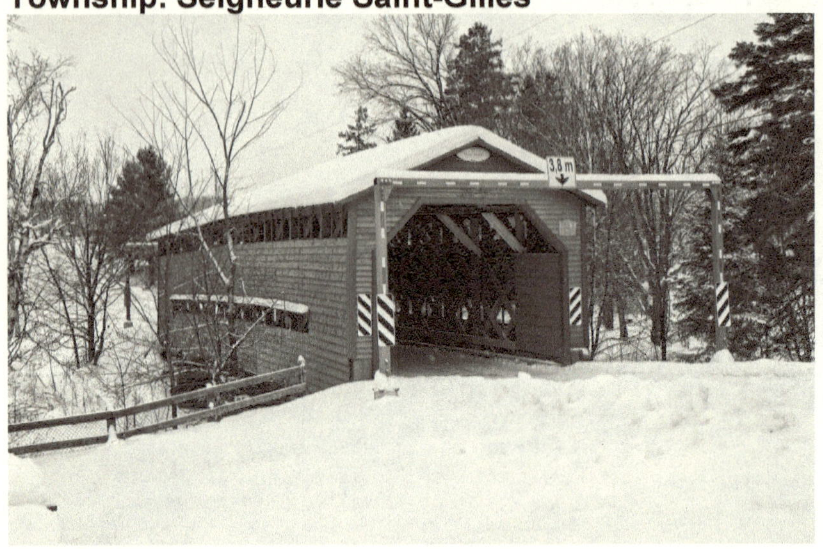

GPS Position: 46°21'34.0"N 71°19'14.0"W
Directions: From Wilson, head west on Rte de Ste Agathe/QC-271 N for 3.5 km and turn right onto Rang St Michel. After 2.5 km continue onto Rang St André/Rte St André and the bridge is 1.2 km
Crosses: Rivière Filkars
Carries: Rang St André/Rte St André
Builder: Not known
Year Built: 1927 (R2002) (R2013)
Truss Type: Town variation
Dimensions: 1 Span, 25 meters, 81 feet
Notes: The bridge was bypassed in 1992 and a picnic area was developed at the site. It was formerly blue-gray but was painted red in 2002
World Index Number: QC/61-40-03
Formerly Listed in County: Lotbinière

Pont Caron

Region: Chaudière-Appalaches
Township: Seigneurie Lotbinière

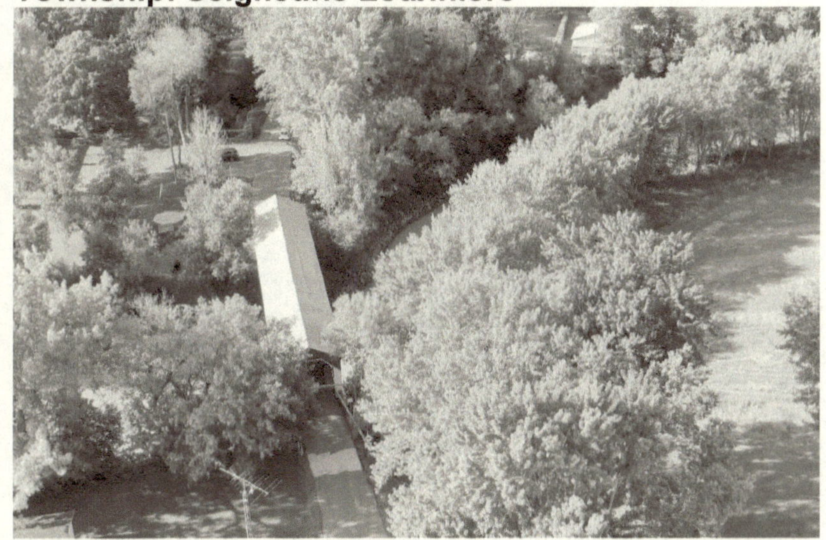

GPS Position: 46°25'19.0"N 71°42'20.0"W
Directions: From Val-Alain, head southeast on Rue de la Station for 1.6 km and continue onto 1er Rang where the bridge is 3.0 km
Crosses: Grande Rivière du Chêne
Carries: 1er Rang
Builder: Romain Caron
Year Built: 1933 or 1942
Truss Type: Town variation
Dimensions: 1 Span, 25 meters, 81 feet
Notes: The bridge is named for the builder, Romain Caron. The bridge was closed to vehicular traffic in 1979. Shortly after the bridge was closed, the roof collapsed due to a high snow load. A park was added in 2013
World Index Number: QC/61-40-04
Formerly Listed in County: Lotbinière

Pont Rouge (Sainte-Agathe)
Region: Chaudière-Appalaches
Township: Nelson

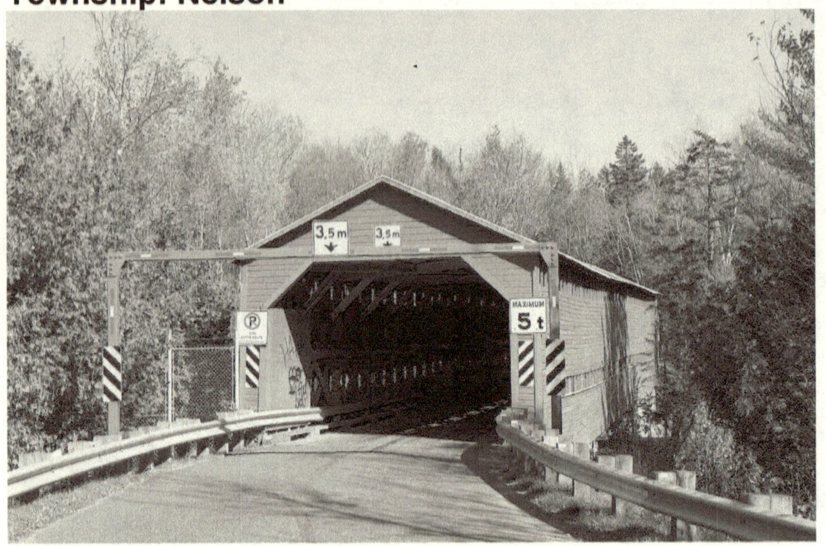

GPS Position: 46°19'50.0"N 71°24'53.0"W
Directions: From Sainte-Agathe, head south on Chem. Gosford/Rue Gosford O for 4.6 km and turn left onto Chem. Gosford where the bridge is 2.6 km
Crosses: Rivière Palmer
Carries: Chem. Gosford
Builder: Not known
Year Built: 1928 (R2007) (2013)
Truss Type: Town variation
Dimensions: 1 Span, 39 meters, 129 feet
Notes: A park has been built at the site which has become very popular. The bridge was restored in 2007. In 2013, height restrictors were added.

World Index Number: QC/61-44-01
Formerly Listed in County: Mégantic

Pont des Défricheurs

Region: Chaudière-Appalaches
Township: Talon

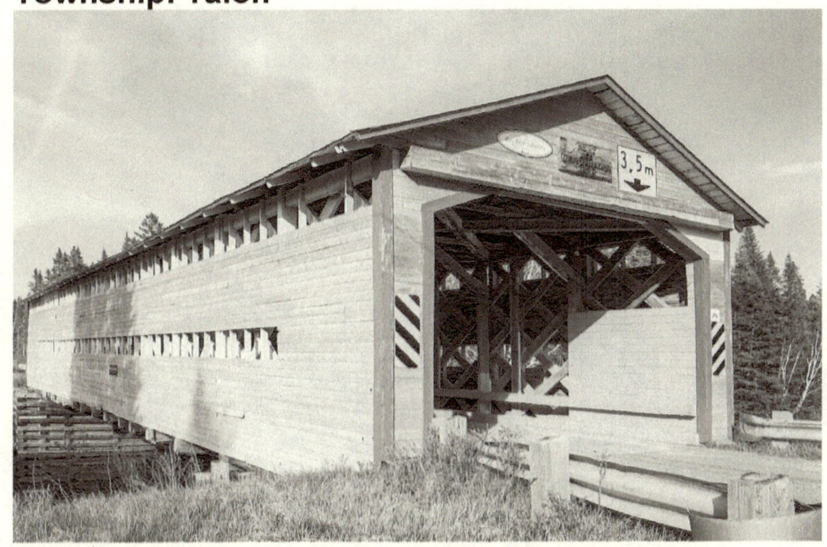

GPS Position: 46°45'15.0"N 70°03'33.0"W
Directions: From Sainte-Lucie-de-Beauregard, head northwest on Rte des Chutes for 3.4 km to find the bridge
Crosses: Rivière Noire Nord-Ouest
Carries: Rte des Chutes
Builder: Not known
Year Built: 1936 (R1970) (R2016)
Truss Type: Town variation
Dimensions: 1 Span, 30 meters, 97 feet
Notes: The bridge was painted orange in the 1970s. The structure was badly damaged in August 2016 and closed to traffic for about 4 months. It was restored and reopened in late 2016. It is named after early settlers

World Index Number: QC/61-47-02
Formerly Listed in County: Montmagny

Pont des Pionniers

Region: Eeyou Istchee Baie-James
Township: Rousseau

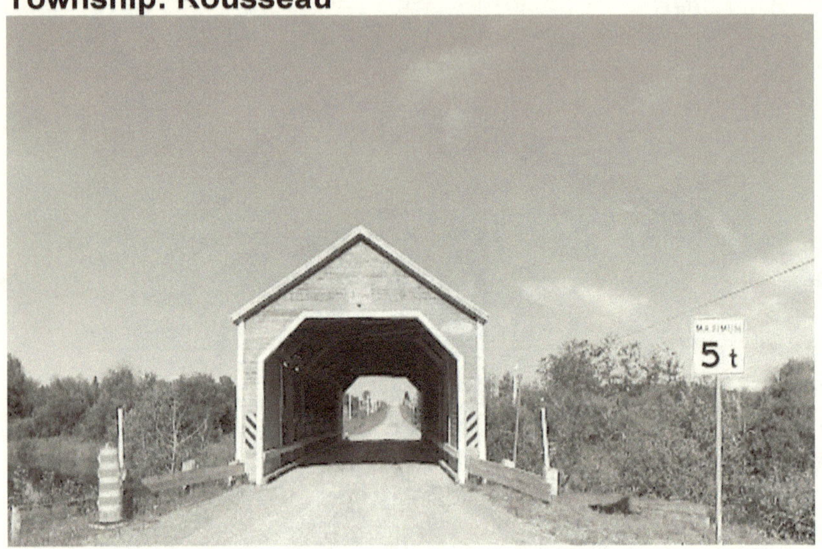

GPS Position: 49°07'35.8"N 79°15'16.6"W
Directions: From Val-Paradis, head east on Chem. des 10e-et-1er-Rangs/QC-393 S for 2.8 km and take a slight right onto QC-393 S, After 3.2 km turn right onto Chem. des 8e et 9e Rangs and the bridge is 1.1 km
Crosses: Ruisseau Leslie
Carries: Chem. des 8e et 9e Rangs
Builder: Ministry of Colonization
Year Built: 1943 (R1985) (R1992)
Truss Type: Town variation
Dimensions: 1 Span, 25 meters, 81 feet
Notes: The bridge is named for the settlers to the area. A restoration was performed in 1985 and the bridge was painted red from its former gray. The roof was replaced in 1992.
World Index Number: QC/61-02-32
Formerly Listed in County: Abitibi-Ouest

Pont des Souvenirs

Region: Eeyou Istchee Baie-James
Township: Rousseau

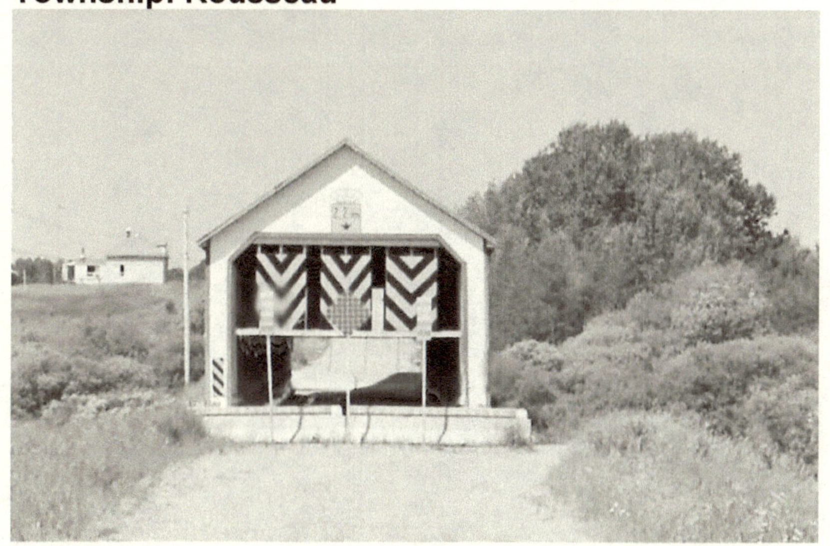

GPS Position: 49°02'18.9"N 79°10'50.9"W
Directions: From Beaucanton, head east on Chem. des 2 et 3 Rangs for 4.2 km where you will see the bridge
Crosses: Rivière Turgeon
Carries: Chem. des 2 et 3 Rangs
Builder: Ministry of Colonization
Year Built: 1954
Truss Type: Town variation
Dimensions: 2 Spans, 44 meters, 145 feet

Notes: In 1995, the maximum load was reduced from 12 tonnes to 5 tonnes. The name honours the first settlers in the area. In 2010 the bridge was closed to vehicular traffic.

World Index Number: QC/61-02-33
Formerly Listed in County: Abitibi-Ouest

Pont Maurice-Duplessis

Region: Eeyou Istchee Baie-James
Township: Rousseau

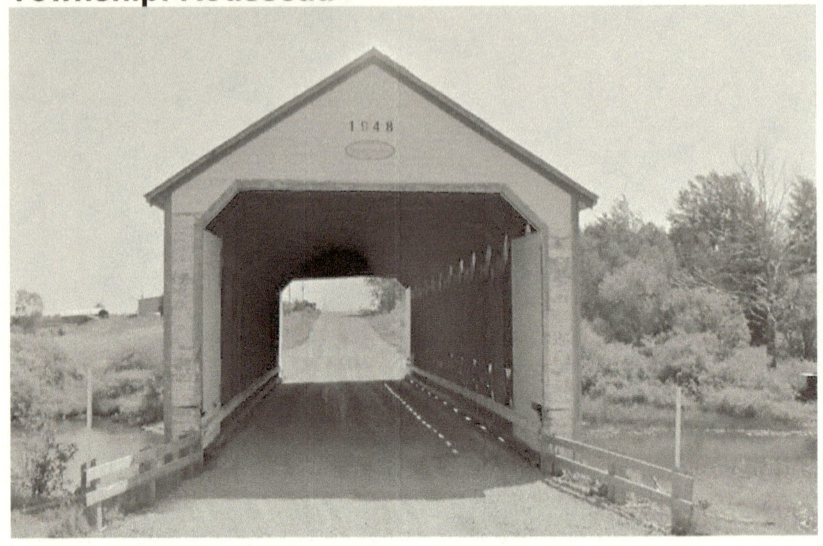

GPS Position: 49°04'04.0"N 79°10'30.0"W
Directions: From Beasucanton, head north on QC-393 N for 3.2 km and turn right onto Chem. des 4 et 5 Rangs. After 4.7 km you will find the bridge
Crosses: Rivière Turgeon
Carries: Chem. des 4 et 5 Rangs
Builder: Ministry of Colonization
Year Built: 1948 (R1984)
Truss Type: Town variation
Dimensions: 1 Span, 30 meters, 97 feet
Notes: A major restoration was performed in 1984 which included modifying the side windows. It was also repainted gray at that time.

World Index Number: QC/61-02-34
Formerly Listed in County: Abitibi-Ouest

Pont Taschereau

Region: Eeyou Istchee Baie-James
Township: Rousseau

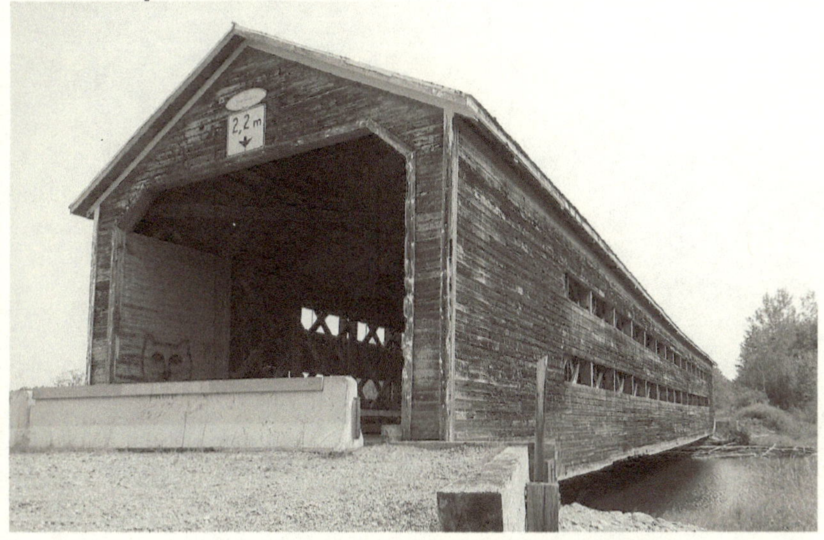

GPS Position: 49°07'35.0"N 79°12'03.0"W
Directions: From Villebois, head north on Rte des Conquérants for 2.8 km and turn left onto Chem. des 8e et 9e Rangs. After 3.9 km you will find the bridge
Crosses: Rivière Turgeon
Carries: Chem. des 8e et 9e Rangs
Builder: Ministry of Colonization
Year Built: 1939
Truss Type: Town variation
Dimensions: 1 Span, 44 meters, 145 feet
Notes: The bridge was named in honour of Louis-Alexandre Taschereau, former Premier of Quebec. It has been closed to traffic since August 2009. The structure was formerly painted red but looks unpainted due to wear.
World Index Number: QC/61-02-39
Formerly Listed in County: Abitibi-Ouest

Pont de Saint-Edgar

Region: Gaspésie
Township: New Richmond

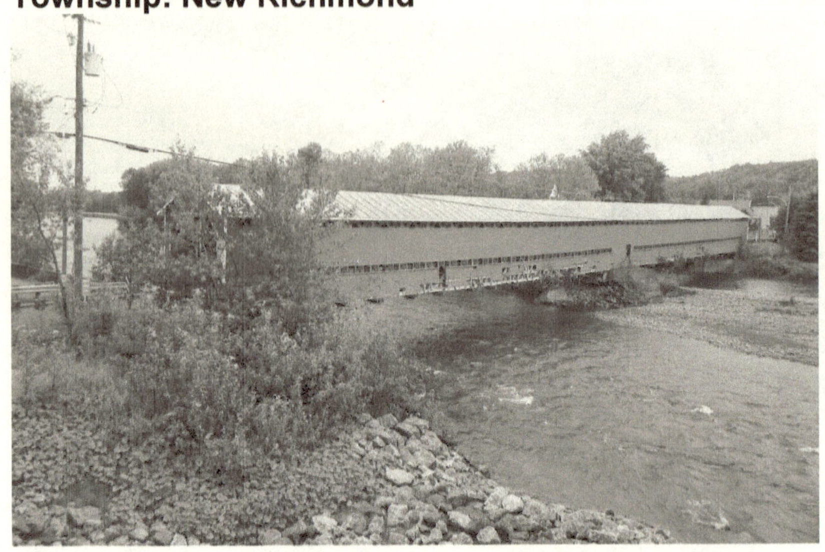

GPS Position: 48°14'15.0"N 65°43'32.0"W
Directions: From Chaleurs, head northeast on Chem. de Saint-Edgar for 11.5 km and turn left onto Rue du Pont where you will see the bridge
Crosses: Petit Rivière Cascapédia
Carries: Rue du Pont
Builder: Not known
Year Built: 1938 (R2014)
Truss Type: Town variation
Dimensions: 2 Spans, 89 meters, 293 feet
Notes: The bridge was painted red in 1980, having previously been gray. The bridge was bypassed and closed to highway traffic in 2008. It was restored in 2014 by Construction LFG

World Index Number: QC/61-10-05
Formerly Listed in County: Bonaventure

Pont Galipeault

Region: Gaspésie

Township: Seigneurie de la Grande-Vallée

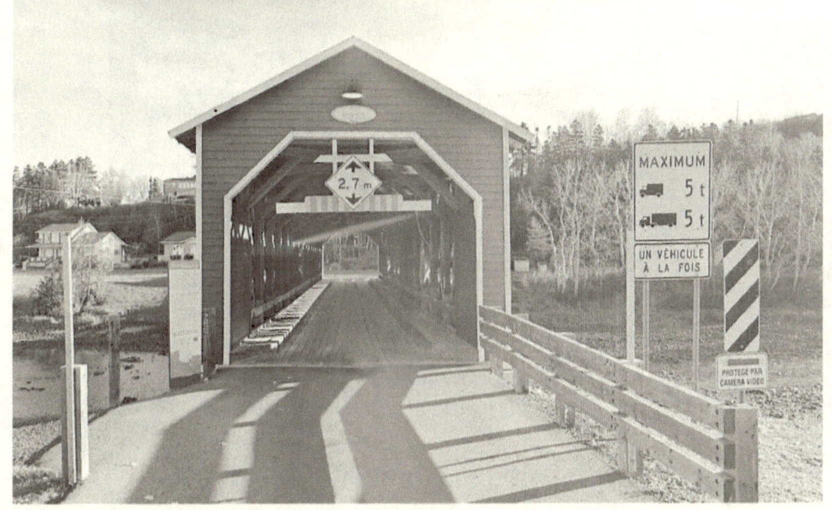

GPS Position: 49°13'21.0"N 65°07'33.0"W

Directions: From Grande-Vallée, head NW on Rue St François Xavier E for 210 m and turn right onto Rue de la Fabrique. After 19 m make a slight right onto Rue du Vieux Pont and the bridge is 400 m

Crosses: Rivière de la Grande-Vallèe

Carries: Rue du Vieux Pont

Builder: Not known

Year Built: 1923 (R1985) (R2016)

Truss Type: Town variation

Dimensions: 1 Span, 44 meters, 145 feet

Notes: Metal support added around 1985 to strengthen the structure. Major restoration work carried out in 2016. It still carries vehicle traffic.

World Index Number: QC/61-23-01

Formerly Listed in County: Gaspé-Nord

Pont Jean-Chassé (St. Luc)

Region: Gaspésie
Township: Tessier

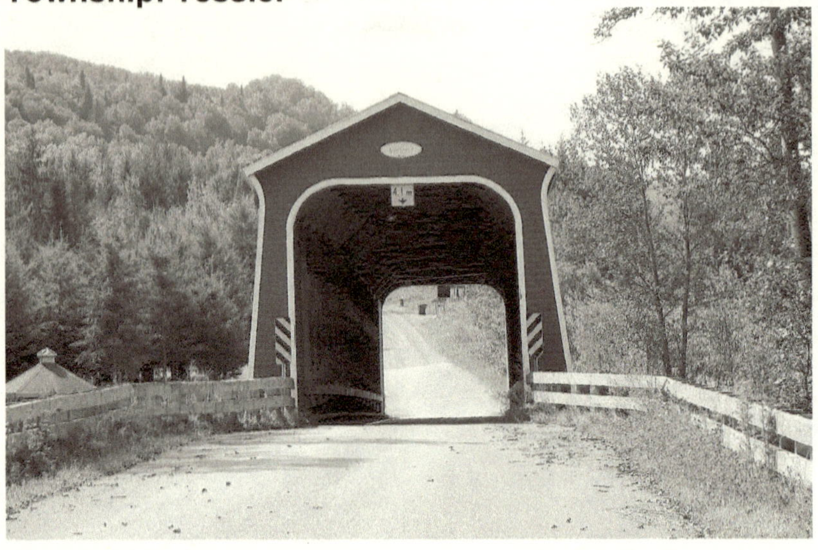

GPS Position: 48°43'12.0"N 67°24'50.0"W
Directions: From Ruisseau-Gagnon, head southwest on Rte de la Montagne and the bridge is found in 110 m
Crosses: Rivière Matane
Carries: Rte de la Montagne
Builder: Not known
Year Built: 1945 (R2000)
Truss Type: Town variation
Dimensions: 1 Span, 44 meters, 145 feet
Notes: This bridge is named for Jean Chassé, the original owner of the land at the site. The bridge was restored in 2000 by company C. J. Picard. At this time a steel bridge was built and the old framework was attached.

World Index Number: QC/61-42-01
Formerly Listed in County: Matane

Pont Bélanger (Les Boules)

Region: Gaspésie
Township: MacNider

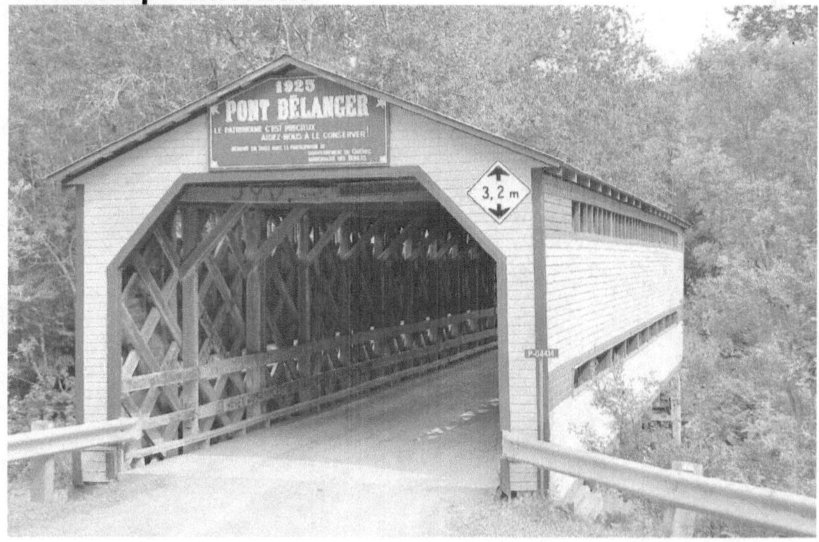

GPS Position: 48°38'08.0"N 67°54'20.0"W
Directions: From MacNider, head SW on Av. Principale for 850 m and turn right onto Rue de l'Église. Continue onto 7e Rang O for 7.0 km and turn right onto Rte Macnider where the site is 2.6 km
Crosses: Rivière Tartigou
Carries: Rte Macnider
Builder: Not known
Year Built: 1925 (R1993) (R2002)
Truss Type: Town variation
Dimensions: 1 Span, 27 meters, 88 feet
Notes: The bridge was damaged in 1992 and repaired by 1993. Repair work in 2002 include replacement of panelling. It was named for a pioneer family.
World Index Number: QC/61-42-04
Formerly Listed in County: Matane

Pont Pierre-Carrier

Region: Gaspésie
Township: Matane

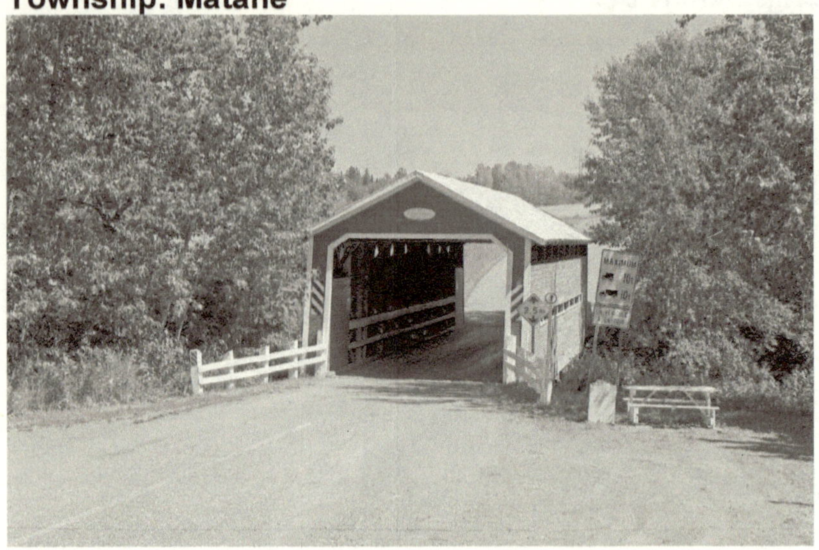

GPS Position: 48°46'20.0"N 67°41'05.0"W
Directions: From Saint-Ulric, head SW on Rte James for 1.9 km and turn left onto Chem. du Pont Couvert where the bridge is 500 m
Crosses: Blanche
Carries: Chem. du Pont Couvert
Builder: Not known
Year Built: 1918 (R2010) (R2016)
Truss Type: Town variation
Dimensions: 1 Span, 25 meters, 81 feet
Notes: The bridge is named for Pierre Carrier, a pioneer of the area. The site was restored in 2010. The portals were damaged in 2016 and repaired the same year.

World Index Number: QC/61-42-05
Formerly Listed in County: Matane

Pont François-Gagnon (Saint-René-de-Matane)

Region: Gaspésie
Township: Tessier

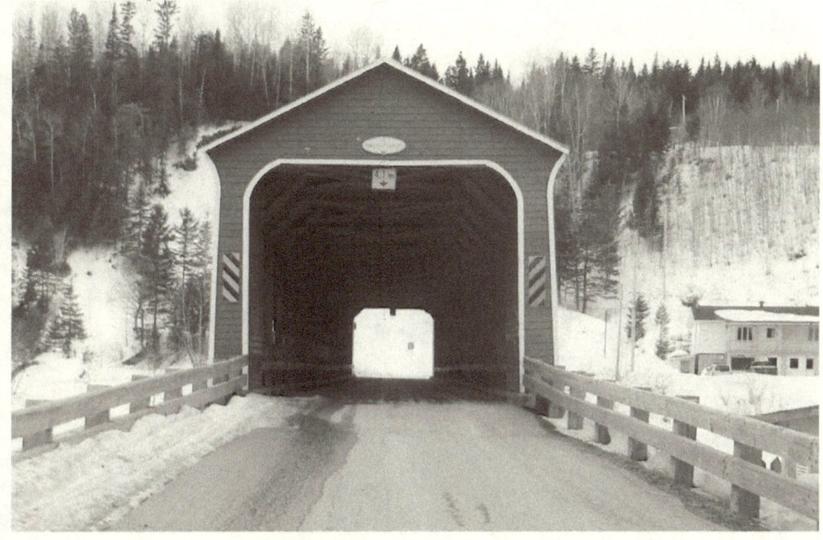

GPS Position: 48°42'24.0"N 67°23'22.0"W
Directions: In Saint-René-de-Matane, head southwest from QC-195 on Rue Degas for a short distance to see the bridge
Crosses: Rivière Matane
Carries: Rue Degas
Builder: Not known
Year Built: 1942 (R1995) (R2018)
Truss Type: Town variation
Dimensions: 1 Span, 52 meters, 170 feet

Notes: In 1995, a steel substructure was added, making the town truss nonfunctional. It was painted red from its former gray, in 1996. It remains open to traffic.

World Index Number: QC/61-42-06
Formerly Listed in County: Matane

Pont Heppell

Region: Gaspésie
Township: Matalik-Casapscull

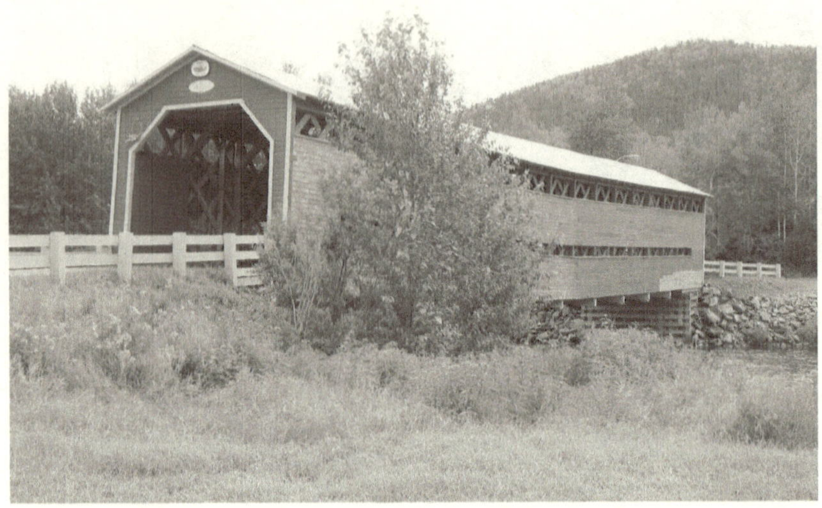

GPS Position: 48°18'43.0"N 67°14'29.0"W
Directions: From the town of Heppell, head west on Rte Heppell from Rte 132 E for a short distance to see the bridge.
Crosses: Rivière Matapédia
Carries: Rte Heppell
Builder: Not known
Year Built: 1909 (R1991) (R2018)
Truss Type: Town variation
Dimensions: 1 Span, 39 meters, 129 feet

Notes: The bridge was badly damaged by a 1991 flood and was repaired the same year. It was hard hit by water again in 2017. It was repaired by the next year.

World Index Number: QC/61-43-02
Formerly Listed in County: Matapédia

Pont de Routhierville

Region: Gaspésie

Township: Milnikek-Assemetquagan

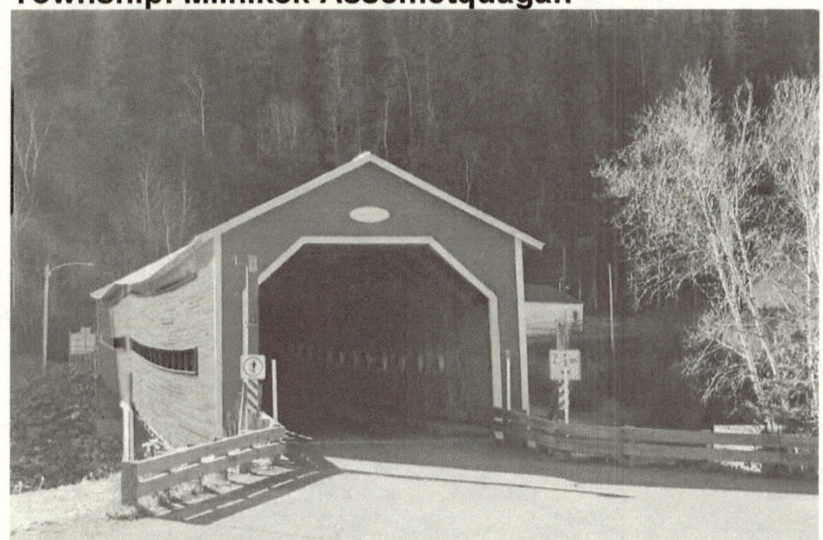

GPS Position: 48°10'56.0"N 67°08'57.0"W

Directions: From Milnikek, head northeast on Chem. du 2 Rang Matalik for 5.7 km and turn right onto Chem. du Rang A where the bridge is 1.9 km

Crosses: Rivière Matapédia

Carries: Chem. du Rang A

Builder: Not known

Year Built: 1931 (R1994) (R2012) (R2021)

Truss Type: Town variation

Dimensions: 2 Spans, 79 meters, 259 feet

Notes: The repairs in 1994 were needed after heavy flood damage. A restoration was done between 2010 and 2012. It was closed for repairs in 2021 and reopened the same year.

World Index Number: QC/61-43-04

Formerly Listed in County: Matapédia

Pont de l'Anse-Saint-Jean (Amqui)

Region: Gaspésie
Township: Seigneurie du lac Matapédia

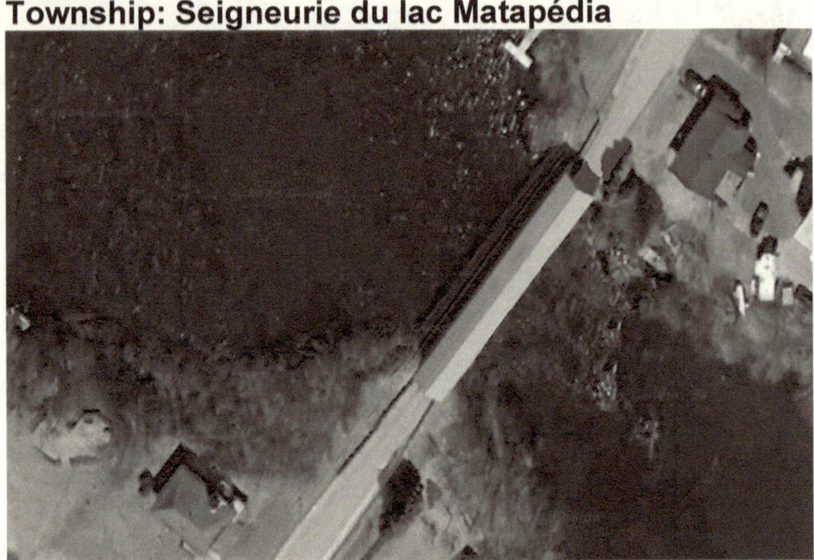

GPS Position: 48°29'31.0"N 67°26'54.0"W
Directions: From Amqui, head west on QC-132 E for 3.3 km and turn right onto Chem. du Pont Couvert where you find the bridge
Crosses: Rivière Matapédia
Carries: Chem. du Pont Couvert
Builder: Not known
Year Built: 1931 (R1970s)
Truss Type: Town variation
Dimensions: 1+ Span, 44 meters, 145 feet
Notes: A center pier was added in the 1950s. It was restored in the 1970s. In 1990 it was decided to demolish the structure but it was saved after local protests.

World Index Number: QC/61-43-05
Formerly Listed in County: Matapédia

Pont Beauséjour

Region: Gaspésie

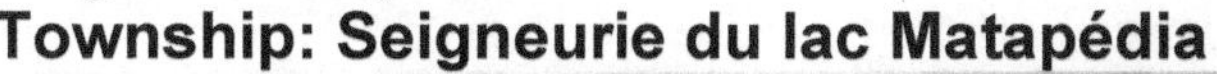

Township: Seigneurie du lac Matapédia

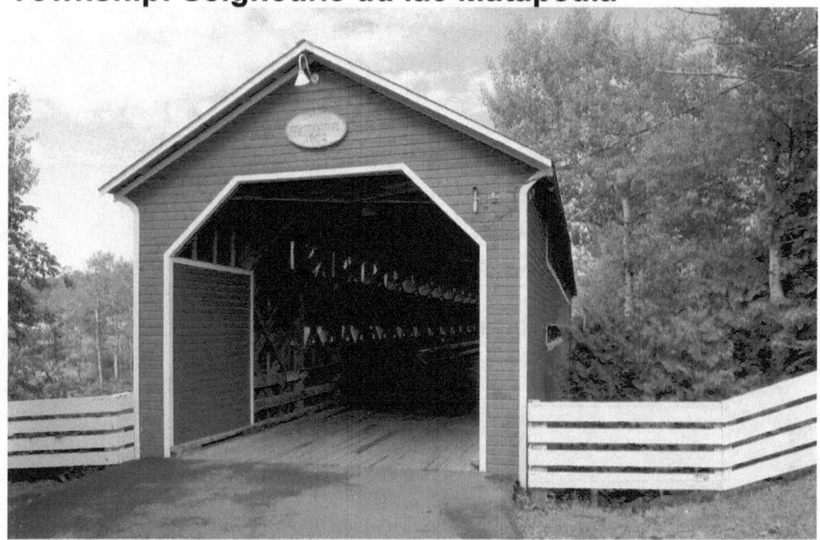

GPS Position: 48°27'58.0"N 67°26'00.0"W
Directions: In Amqui, head northeast on Rue du Pont from 132 for 250 m and turn left onto Rue Desbiens. After 200 m turn left onto Rue Ste Ursule where you see the bridge
Crosses: Rivière Matapédia
Carries: Rue Ste Ursule
Builder: Not known
Year Built: 1932 (M2005)
Truss Type: Town variation
Dimensions: 1 Span, 37 meters, 122 feet
Notes: The bridge was removed from its original location in Rimouski County in 2003 and was reconstructed in a public park in Amqui in 2005

World Index Number: QC/61-43-25
Formerly Listed in County: Matapédia

Pont Grandchamp

Region: Lanaudière

Township: Seigneurie Berthier

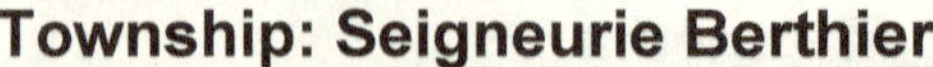

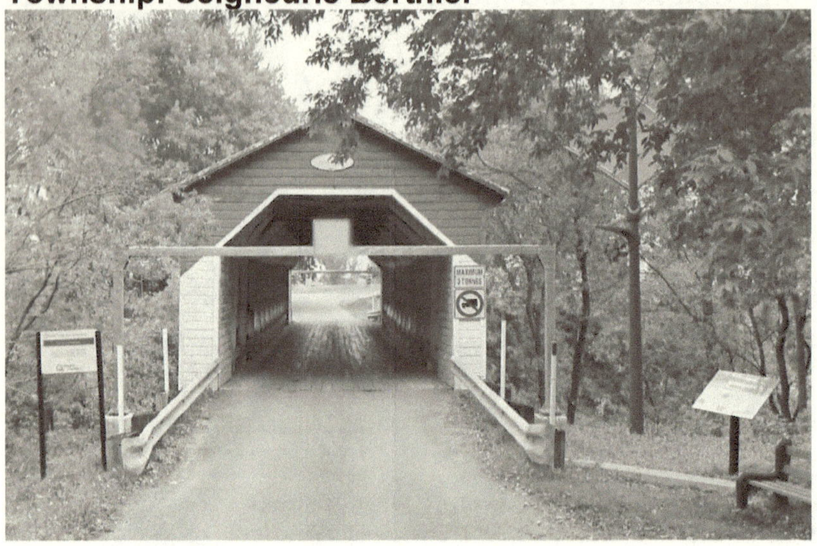

GPS Position: 46°05'35.4"N 73°12'41.0"W
Directions: From Berthierville, head northwest on Bd Gilles Villeneuve/QC-158 O for 2.3 km
Crosses: Rivière Berthier
Carries: Bd Gilles Villeneuve/QC-158 O
Builder: Not known
Year Built: c.1918 (R1996) (R1998)
Truss Type: Town variation
Dimensions: 1 Span, 34 meters, 113 feet

Notes: The bridge was closed to traffic in 1977. Steel beams were installed in 1966 and the bridge was reopened. In 1998 the roof was repaired and the bridge was repainted

World Index Number: QC/61-09-02
Formerly Listed in County: Berthier

Grand pont de Ferme Rouge

Region: Laurentides
Township: Bouthillier - Kiamika

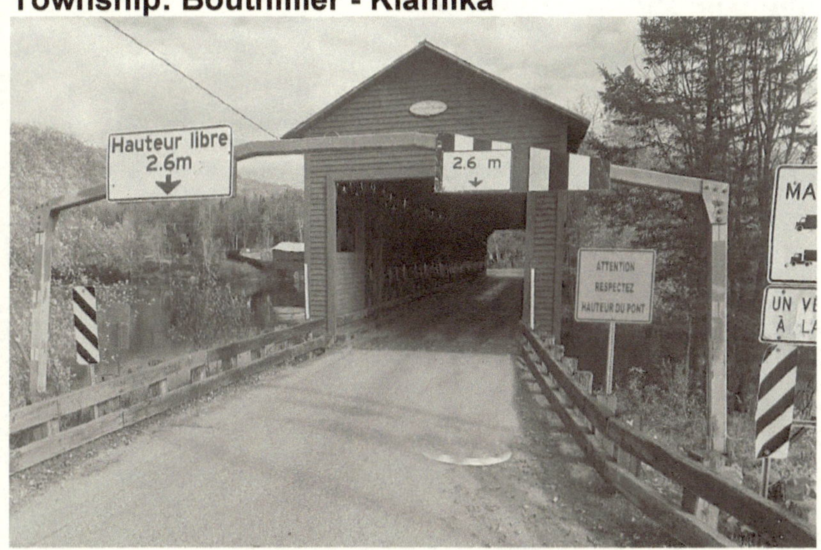

GPS Position: 46°25'35.0"N 75°25'44.5"W
Directions: From Kiamika, head northwest on Chem. de Frm Rouge for 3.7 km and turn right onto Chem. de Frm Rouge. In 600 m turn left onto Chem. de Kiamika and the bridge
Crosses: Rivière du Lièvre
Carries: Chem. de Kiamika
Builder: Not known
Year Built: 1903
Truss Type: Town variation
Dimensions: 2 Spans, 77 meters, 251 feet
Notes: This is the longer of a pair of bridges at this site. It was closed for a few days in spring 2018 and spring 2019 due to flooding.

World Index Number: QC/61-33-02
Formerly Listed in County: Labelle

Petit pont de Ferme Rouge
Region: Laurentides
Township: Bouthillier - Kiamika

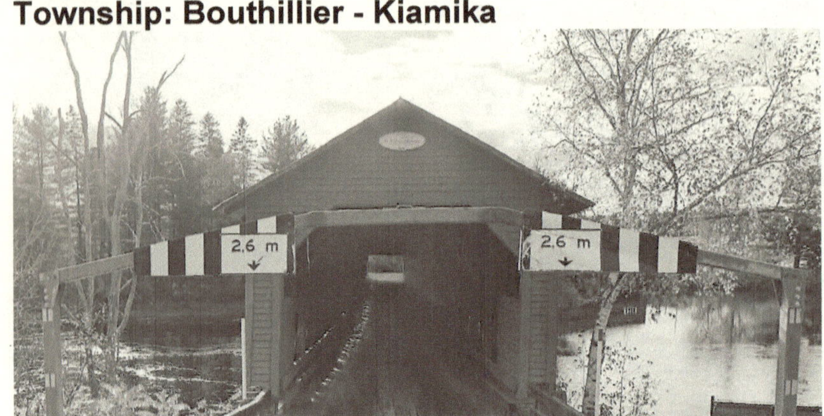

GPS Position: 46°25'35.1"N 75°25'40.0"W
Directions: From Kiamika, head northwest on Chem. de Frm Rouge for 3.7 km and turn right onto Chem. de Frm Rouge. In 600 m turn left onto Chem. de Kiamika and the bridge
Crosses: Rivière du Lièvre
Carries: Chem. de Kiamika
Builder: Not known
Year Built: 1903
Truss Type: Town variation
Dimensions: 2 Span, 49 meters, 162 feet
Notes: This is the shorter of a pair of bridges at this site. It was closed for a few days in spring 2018 and spring 2019 due to flooding.

World Index Number: QC/61-33-03
Formerly Listed in County: Labelle

Pont Armand Lachaîne

Region: Laurentides
Township: Rochon-Moreau

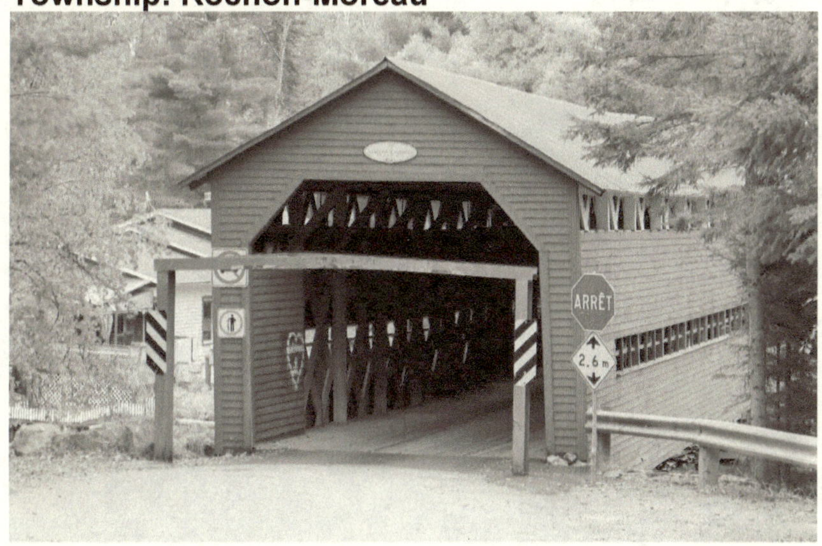

GPS Position: 46°38'36.0"N 75°16'08.0"W
Directions: From Lac-Saint-Paul, head south on QC-311 S for 12.2 km and turn right onto Chem. du Progrès for 280 m. Turn left onto Chem. du Vieux Pont and the bridge
Crosses: Rivière Kiamika
Carries: Chem. du Vieux Pont
Builder: Not known
Year Built: 1904 (R2024)
Truss Type: Town variation
Dimensions: 1 Span, 35 meters, 113 feet
Notes: The structure was closed to all vehicle traffic after an accident occurred in May 2024 but was reopened shortly. The bridge was painted red in 2007, from the former white

World Index Number: QC/61-33-05
Formerly Listed in County: Labelle

Pont Macaza

Region: Laurentides
Township: Marchand

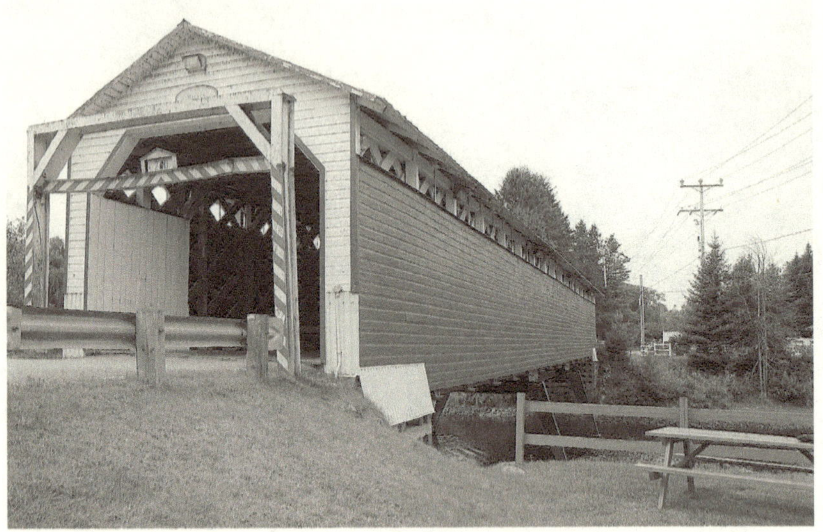

GPS Position: 46°21'24.0"N 74°46'46.0"W
Directions: From Macaza, head east on Chem. des Cascades for 400 m and turn left onto Chem. du Pont Couvert to find the bridge
Crosses: Rivière Macaza
Carries: Chem. du Pont Couvert
Builder: Not known
Year Built: 1904 (R1993) (R2016)
Truss Type: Town variation
Dimensions: 1+ Span, 39 meters, 129 feet
Notes: The bridge was raised and repainted in 1993. There is a picnic table and parking at the site. It underwent a restoration in 2016.

World Index Number: QC/61-33-10
Formerly Listed in County: Labelle

Pont Prud'homme
Region: Laurentides
Township: de Salaberry

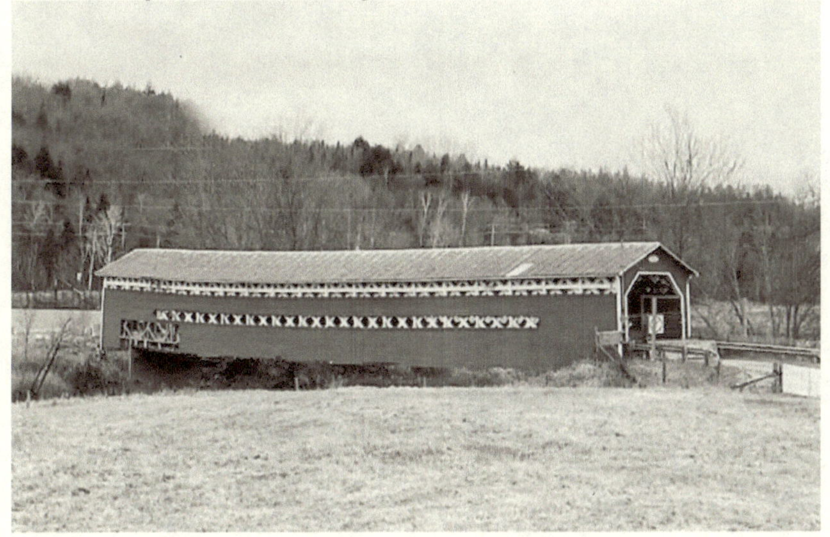

GPS Position: 46°04'22.0"N 74°37'30.0"W
Directions: From Crystal Falls, head northwest on QC-327 N for 2.7 km and turn left onto Chem. du Pont Prud'homme where the bridge is a short distance
Crosses: du Diable
Carries: Chem. du Pont Prud'homme
Builder: Not known
Year Built: 1918 (R1997)
Truss Type: Town variation
Dimensions: 1 Span, 44 meters, 145 feet
Notes: The bridge was restored in 1997 and painted red at that time. It was closed to all traffic in 2019. The site has parking and picnic tables.

World Index Number: QC/61-72-01
Formerly Listed in County: Terrebonne

Pont Louis-Gravel

Region: Manicougan
Township: Albert

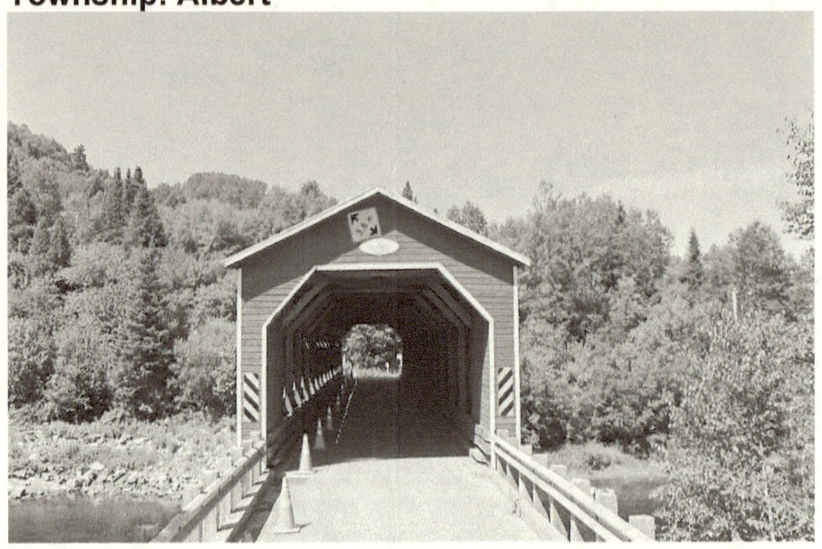

GPS Position: 48°16'04.0"N 69°54'31.0"W
Directions: From Rivière Sainte-Marguerite, head northwest on QC-172 O for 3.4 km and turn left onto Chem. du Vieux-Pont. After 450 m turn left to stay on Chem. du Vieux-Pont and you will see the bridge
Crosses: Rivière Sainte-Marguerite Nord-Est
Carries: Chem. du Vieux-Pont
Builder: Not known
Year Built: 1934 (R1999) (R2012)
Truss Type: Town variation
Dimensions: 1 Span, 39 meters, 129 feet
Notes: The bridge collapsed in 1998 and needed major repair, which was completed in 1999. This included adding steel beams. In 2012, repairs were needed due to flood damage
World Index Number: QC/61-62-01
Formerly Listed in County: Saguenay

Pont-Émile Lapointe

Region: Manicougan
Township: Manicougan

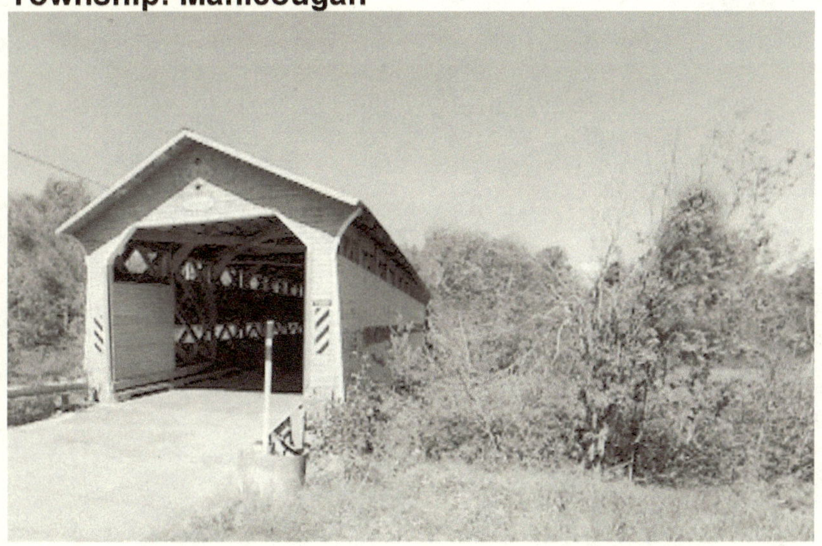

GPS Position: 49°05'41.0"N 68°18'38.0"W
Directions: From Baie-Saint-Ludger, head northeast on Chem. de la Baie Saint-Ludger/Rue de Baie St Ludger for 600 m to find the bridge
Crosses: Rivière Saint-Athanase Ouest
Carries: Rue de Baie St Ludger
Builder: Not known
Year Built: 1945 (R1992)
Truss Type: Town variation
Dimensions: 1 Span, 32 meters, 105 feet
Notes: Built in St. Laudger in 1945, this bridge is named for the owner of the sawmill who provided the wood for construction. A major restoration was completed in 1992

World Index Number: QC/61-62-03
Formerly Listed in County: Saguenay

Pont Bordeleau

Region: Mauricie

Township: Seigneurie Batiscan

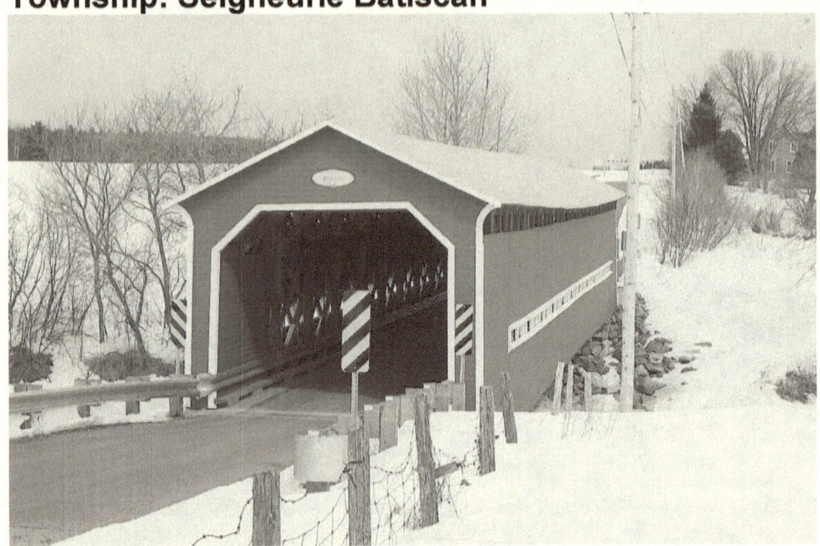

GPS Position: 46°40'24.0"N 72°33'28.0"W

Directions: From Saint-Séverin, head southwest on Rue St Georges for 2.1 km and continue onto Chem. de la Rivière des Envies So/Rang S where the bridge is 2.8 km

Crosses: Rivière des Envies

Carries: Chem. de la Rivière des Envies So/Rang S

Builder: Not known

Year Built: 1932 (R2002) (R2010)

Truss Type: Town variation

Dimensions: 1 Span, 33 meters, 109 feet

Notes: The bridge was closed to traffic in 2001 but reopened after 2002 repairs. It was repaired again in 2010, but closed again in 2017. The bridge is now red with white trim previous to being white with green trim

World Index Number: QC/61-13-03

Formerly Listed in County: Champlain

Pont Ducharme (Saint-Jean Bosco)

Region: Mauricie
Township: Bourgeoys

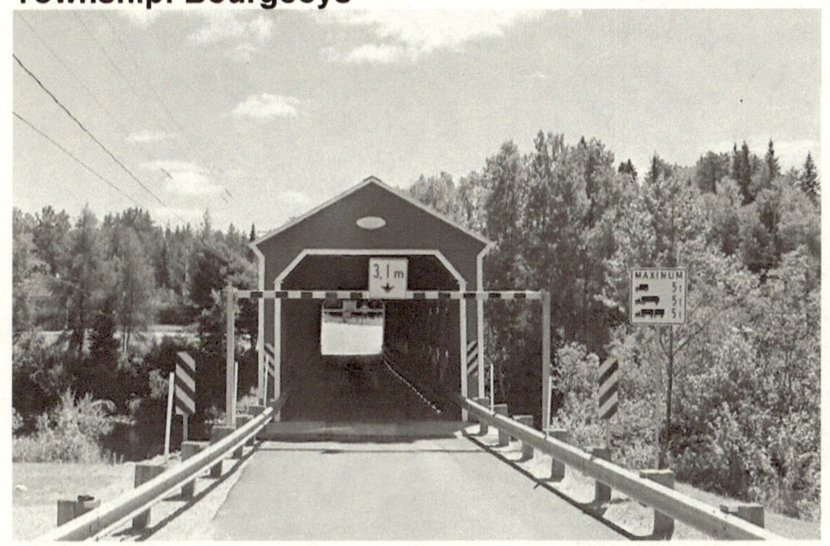

GPS Position: 47°31'11.0"N 72°40'51.0"W
Directions: From La Tuque, head northeast on Rue de la Rivière for 750 m and turn left onto QC-155 N. After 9.9 km turn right onto Rue de l'Église and the bridge
Crosses: Rivière Saint-Athanase Ouest
Carries: Rue de l'Église
Builder: Not known
Year Built: 1946 (R1997) (R2009)
Truss Type: Town variation
Dimensions: 1 Span, 42 meters, 137 feet
Notes: The Bridge is named for Charles Ducharme who was Member of Parliament. It was restored in 1997, when its colour was changed from white to red. It underwent another restoration in 2009
World Index Number: QC/61-62-03
Formerly Listed in County: Laviolette

Pont Thiffault

Region: Mauricie

Township: Bourgeoys

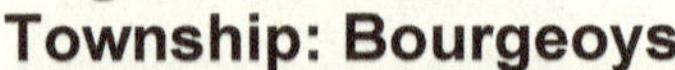

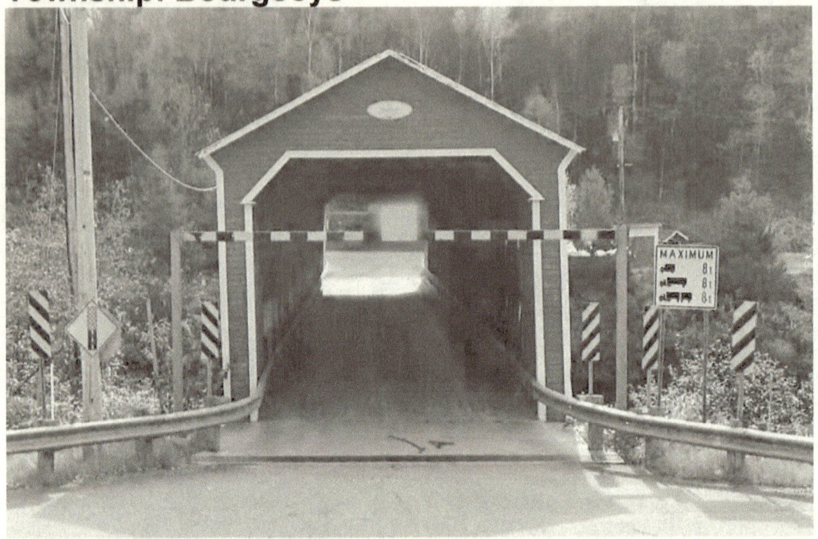

GPS Position: 47°33'45.0"N 72°38'15.0"W
Directions: From La Bostonnais, head north on Rang Bostonnais/Rang Sud-Est for 1.1 km and turn left onto Rue de l'Église. After 450 m turn right onto QC-155 N and travel 6.1 km. Turn right onto Rang Bostonnais and see the bridge
Crosses: Rivière Bostonnais
Carries: Rang Bostonnais
Builder: Raymond Thiffault
Year Built: 1946 (R2009)
Truss Type: Town variation
Dimensions: 1 Span, 42 meters, 137 feet
Notes: The name of the bridge commemorates its builder, Raymond Thiffault. It was painted in red in 2009 after being pale green for many years
World Index Number: QC/61-37-03
Formerly Listed in County: Laviolette

Pont de Saint-Mathieu

Region: Mauricie
Township: Saint-Mathieu

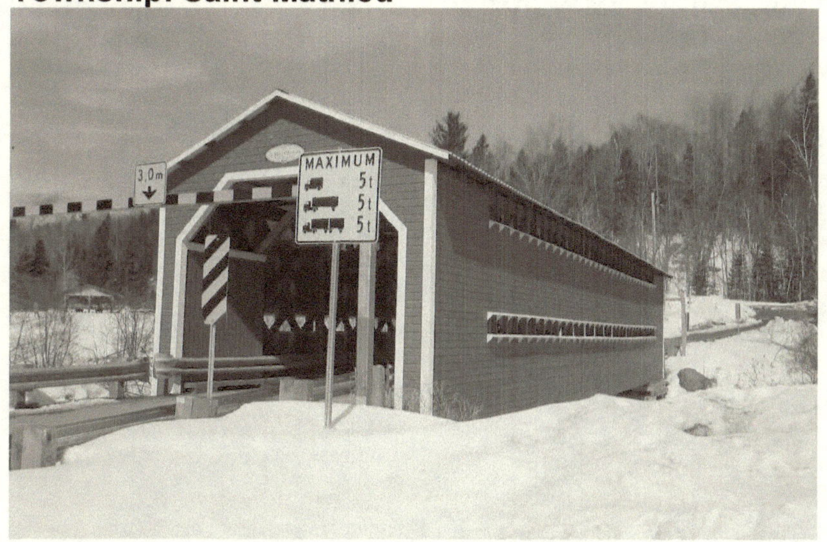

GPS Position: 46°36'10.0"N 72°53'02.0"W
Directions: From Saint-Gérard-des-Laurentides, head SW on QC-351 S for 5.5 km and turn right on Chemin St François. In 700 m, turn right on Chemin du Pont-Couvert and the bridge
Crosses: Rivière Shawinigan
Carries: Chemin du Pont-Couvert
Builder: Not known
Year Built: 1936 (R1974) (R1992) (R2009)
Truss Type: Town variation
Dimensions: 1 Span, 25 meters, 81 feet
Notes: The abutments were repaired and the panelling was repainted in 1974. The abutments were again rebuilt in 1992, when the deck was also replaced. An additional renovation was done in 2009.
World Index Number: QC/61-65-01
Formerly Listed in County: Saint-Maurice

Pont Powerscourt
Region: Montérégie
Township: Elgin-Hinchinbrook

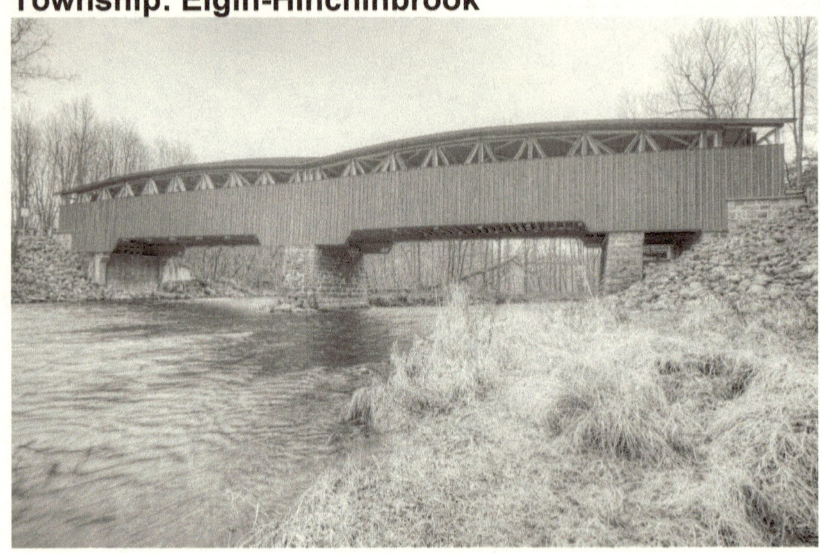

GPS Position: 45°00'25.0"N 74°09'40.0"W
Directions: From Powerscourt, head west on Chem. de la 1e Concession and the bridge is 120 m
Crosses: Rivière Châteauguay
Carries: Chem. de la 1e Concession
Builder: Robert Graham
Year Built: 1933 (R1949) (R1988)
Truss Type: McCallum
Dimensions: 2 Spans, 50 meters, 165 feet
Notes: The author's image above was featured on a Canadian postage stamp in 2019. In 1983 the Ministère des Transports planned to replace the bridge with a concrete one but the local community saved it. It is the only bridge with a McCallum truss

World Index Number: QC/61-27-01
Formerly Listed in County: Huntingdon

Pont Marois

Region: Outaouais
Township: Northfield

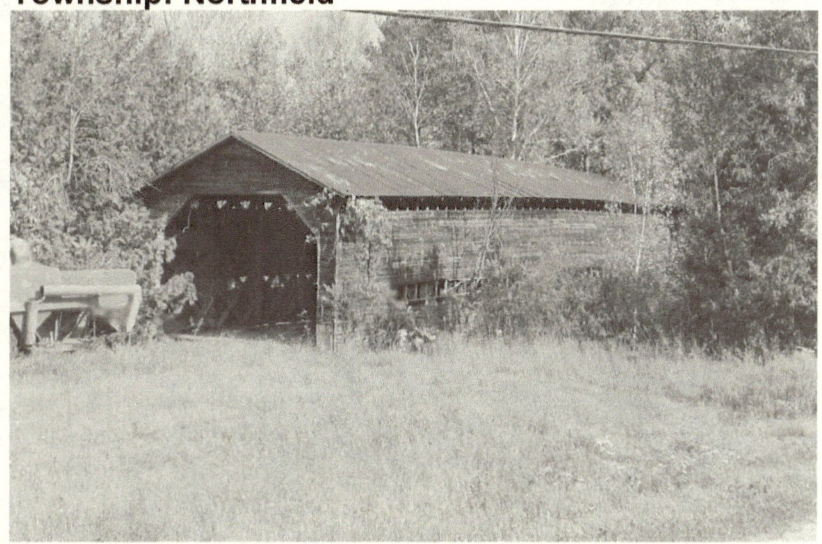

GPS Position: 46°07'07.5"N 75°56'37.1"W
Directions: From Clément, head west on Chem. de Point Comfort for 600 m to find the bridge
Crosses: affluent de la Gatineau
Carries: Chem. de Point Comfort
Builder: Not known
Year Built: 1933
Truss Type: Town variation
Dimensions: 1 Span, 30 meters, 97 fee5

Notes: This bridge closed in 1966 and was purchased by the Marois family who have lived in the area for many years. It is on private property although they seem open to visitors

World Index Number: QC/61-25-02
Formerly Listed in County: Gatineau

Pont Gendrone (Wakefield)
Region: Outaouais
Township: Wakefield

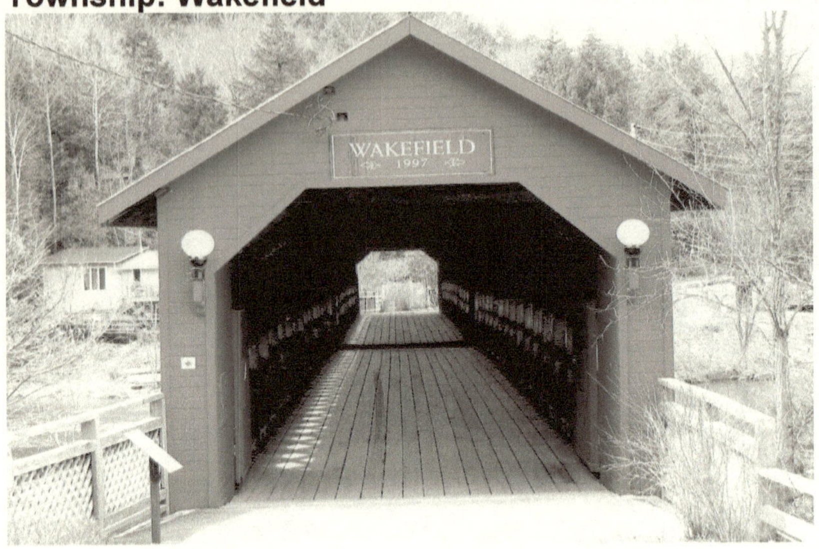

GPS Position: 45°38'44.6"N 75°55'06.2"W
Directions: From Wakefield, head north on Chem. Riverside for 950 m and turn right onto Ch Edelweiss. After 450 m turn right on Chem. de Wakefield Heights and the bridge is 500 m
Crosses: Rivière Gatineau
Carries: Chem. de Wakefield Heights
Builder: Local volunteers
Year Built: 1998
Truss Type: Town variation
Dimensions: 2 Span, 89 meters, 389 feet
Notes: The first covered bridge was built at this site in 1915 and burned down in 1984. Local volunteers proposed rebuilding it for pedestrians and cyclists and it was completed in 1998
World Index Number: QC/61-25-07#2
Formerly Listed in County: Gatineau

Pont Cousineau

Region: Outaouais
Township: Wright

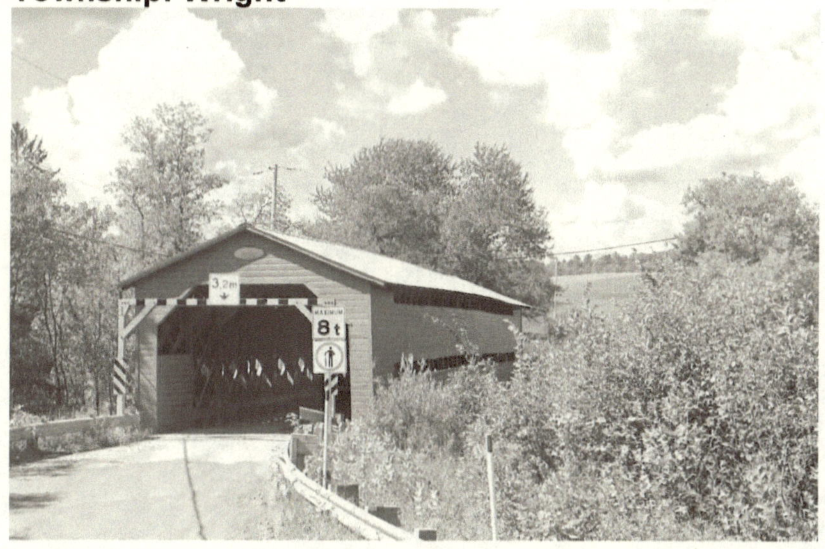

GPS Position: 46°03'57.0"N 76°06'27.0"W
Directions: From Wright County, head west on Chem. du Lac Cayamant for 750 m.Turn left onto Chem. Marks. After 1.1 km turn right on Chem. du Ruisseau des Cerises and the bridge
Crosses: Rivière Picanoc
Carries: Chem. du Ruisseau des Cerises
Builder: Cousineau family
Year Built: 1932 (R1983) (R1995) (R2011)
Truss Type: Town variation
Dimensions: 1 Span, 29 meters, 97 feet
Notes: The name of this bridge honours the memory of the family that built it. In 1995 the bridge was painted white from its former gray. It was completely restored in 2011.

World Index Number: QC/61-25-08
Formerly Listed in County: Gatineau

Pont de l' Aigle

Region: Outaouais

Township: Egan

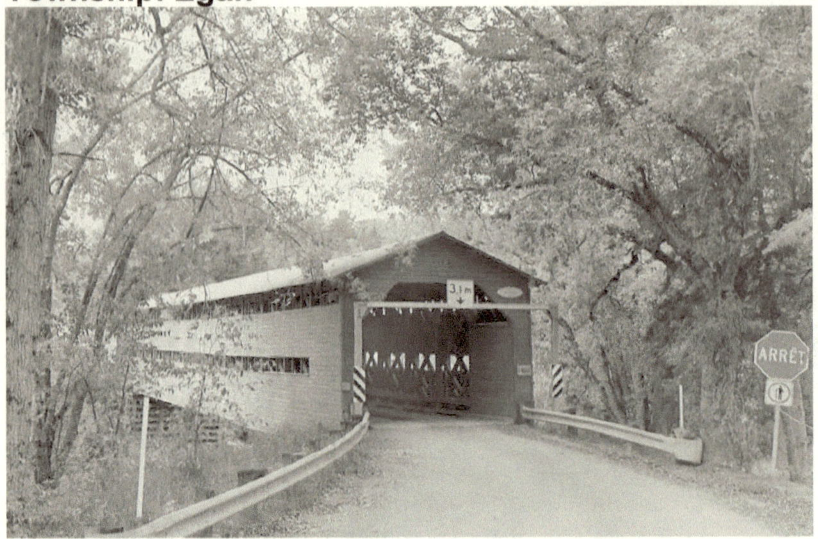

GPS Position: 46°27'10.0"N 76°02'41.0"W

Directions: From Maniwaki, head SW on Rue l'Heureux 260 m and turn right onto Chem. Montcerf. After 9.1 km, continue straight onto Chem. de l'Aigle and the bridge

Crosses: Rivière Désert

Carries: Chem. de l'Aigle

Builder: Not known

Year Built: 1925 (R1986) (R2021)

Truss Type: Town variation

Dimensions: 1 Span, 39 meters, 129 feet

Notes: The bridge is named for the road its on as well as a nearby waterway. In 1986, repairs included painting the panelling red and the roof green. The bridge was closed for a few days in May 2019 due to a flood.

World Index Number: QC/61-25-11

Formerly Listed in County: Gatineau

Pont Ruisseau-Meech

Region: Outaouais
Township: Hull

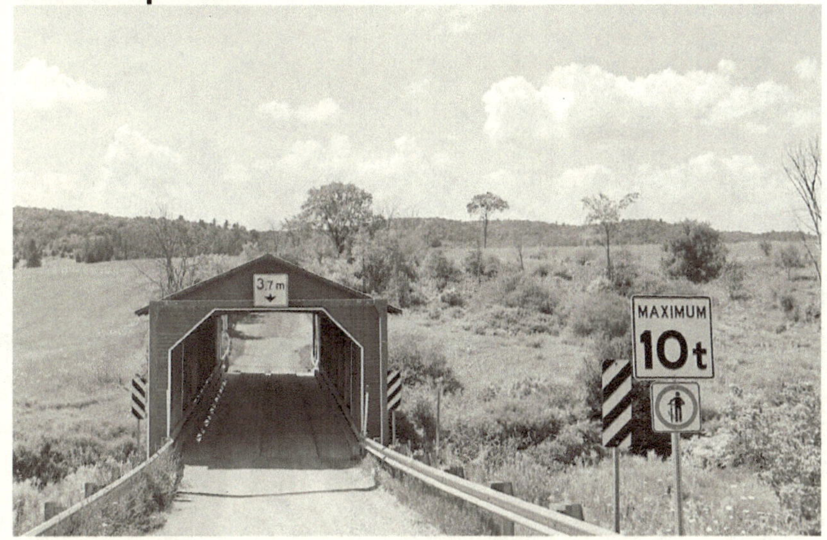

GPS Position: 45°34'57.0"N 75°53'45.0"W
Directions: From Chemin-des-Pins, head west on Chem. Pine for 190 m and turn right onto Rte 105 N and then left onto Chem. Pine. After 900 m turn right onto Chem. Cross Loop and the bridge is 0.4 km
Crosses: Ruisseau-Meech
Carries: Chem. Cross Loop
Builder: Not known
Year Built: 1924 (R1991) (R2010)
Truss Type: Town variation
Dimensions: 1 Span, 19 meters, 65 feet
Notes: A major restoration took place in 2010. The bridge was not accessible in 2018-2019 after being closed to traffic following the collapse of a culvert on the road.
World Index Number: QC/61-25-12
Formerly Listed in County: Gatineau

Pont Savoyard (Grand-Remous)

Region: Outaouais
Township: Lytton/Sicotte

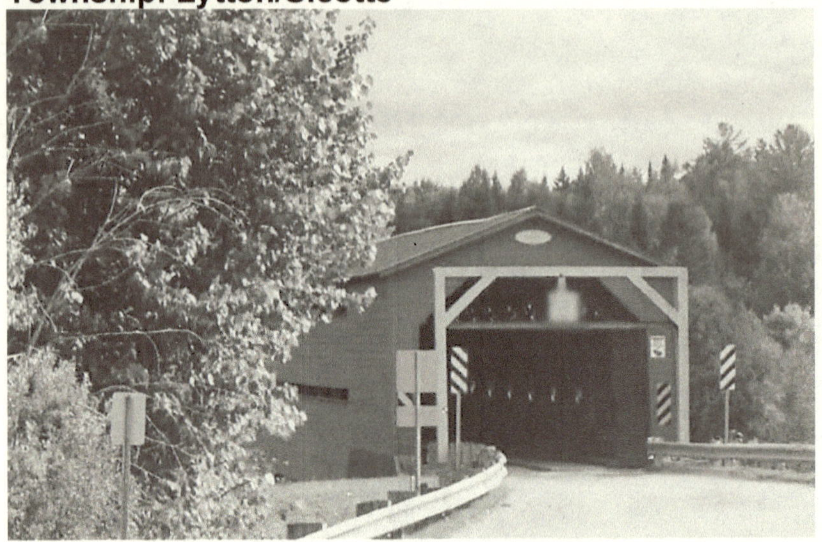

GPS Position: 46°35'30.0"N 75°55'48.0"W
Directions: From Grand-Remous, head south on Rte 105 S for 3.4 km and turn left onto Chem. Pont Rouge where the bridge is 260 m
Crosses: Rivière Gatineau
Carries: Chem. Pont Rouge
Builder: Not known
Year Built: 1925 (R1972)
Truss Type: Town variation
Dimensions: 2+ Spans, 103 meters, 338 feet
Notes: In 1972, a flood damaged the bridge but was quickly repaired. In 1998, the municipality created a rest area at the site with picnic tables and parking. The structure was restored in the summer of 2011
World Index Number: QC/61-25-15
Formerly Listed in County: Gatineau

Pont Brabant-Philippe

Region: Outaouais
Township: Gatineau

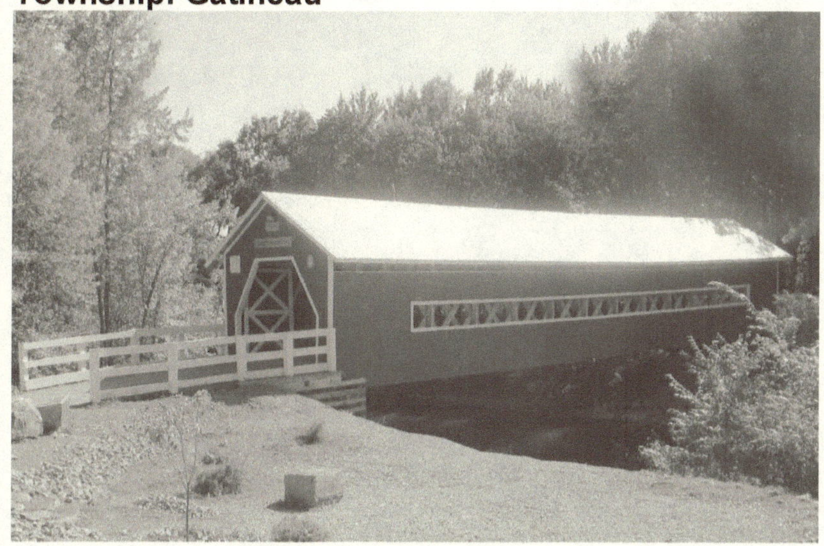

GPS Position: 45°29'54.0"N 75°35'39.0"W
Directions: From Gatineau, head north on QC-366 O for 700 m and turn right onto Rue Sainte-Rose. After 900 m turn left onto Rue Robert Corbett,then right to the bridge
Crosses: Rivière Blanche
Carries: Rue Leclerc
Builder: Construction FGK
Year Built: 2020
Truss Type: Town variation
Dimensions: 1 Span, 31 meters, 108 feet
Notes: This is the third bridge at this location. The first one was lost to arson in 2011. The second was completed in 2015 but burned again in 2016. The current bridge was built by Construction FGK and opened in 2020.
World Index Number: QC/61-25-34#3
Formerly Listed in County: Gatineau

Pont Roland-Houét

Region: Outaouais
Township: Gatineau

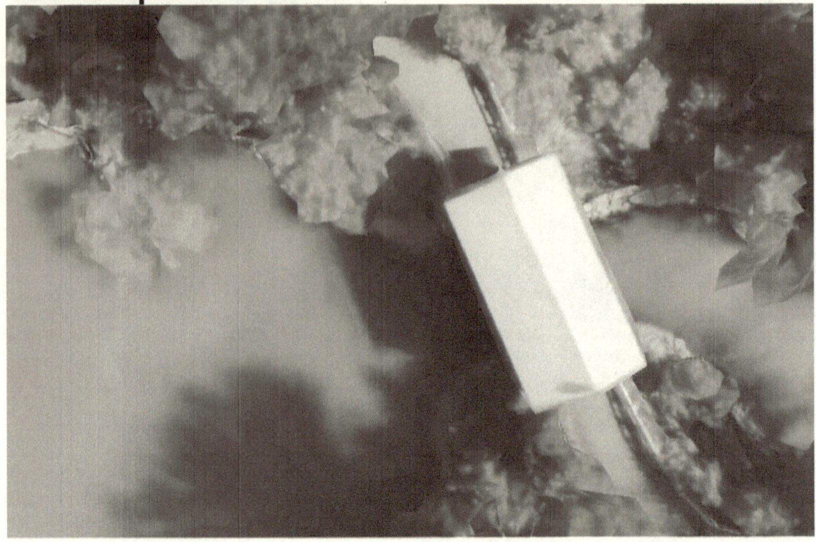

GPS Position: 45°29'59.5"N 75°36'16.3"W
Directions: From Gatineau, head north on Bd Lorrain/QC-366 O for 210 m and turn right onto Rue Vincent-Legris where the bridge is a short walk
Crosses: Rivière Blanche
Carries: N/A
Builder: Not known
Year Built: 2009
Truss Type: Town variation
Dimensions: 1 Span, 12 meters, 40 feet
Notes: This bridge was built on the White River trail for pedestrians and cyclists. It is the second covered bridge on the trail with plans for two more.

World Index Number: QC/61-25-35
Formerly Listed in County: Gatineau

Pont des Bénévoles

Region: Outaouais
Township: Gatineau

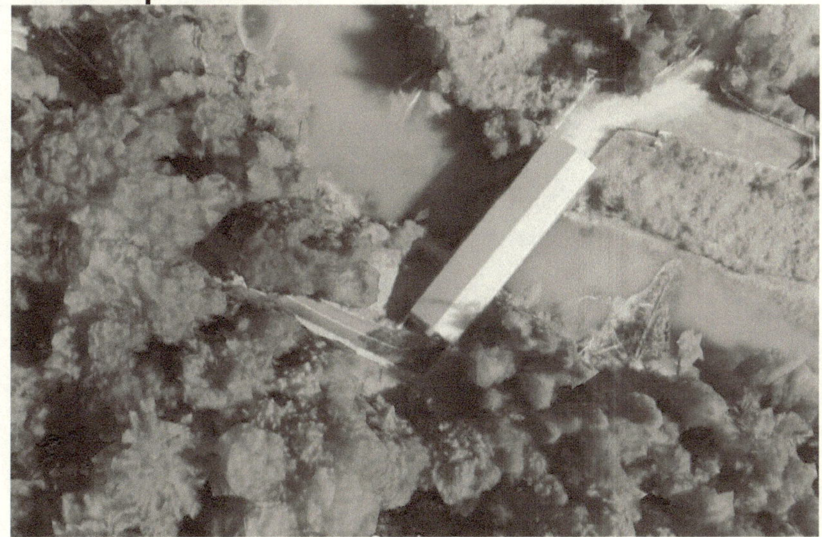

GPS Position: 45°30'11.2"N 75°36'02.0"W
Directions: In Gatineau, head north on Bd Lorrain/QC-366 O for 850 m and turn right onto Rue des Fleurs. After 600 m turn left onto Rue des Jacinthes where the bridge is 350 m
Crosses: Rivière Blanche
Carries: N/A
Builder: Not known
Year Built: 2016
Truss Type: Town variation
Dimensions: 1 Span, 28 meters, 92 feet
Notes: This bridge was built on the White River trail for pedestrians and cyclists. It is the third covered bridge on the trail with plans for one more. It was named for the volunteers

World Index Number: QC/61-25-36
Formerly Listed in County: Gatineau

Pont Félix-Gabriel-Marchand
Region: Outaouais
Township: Mansfield

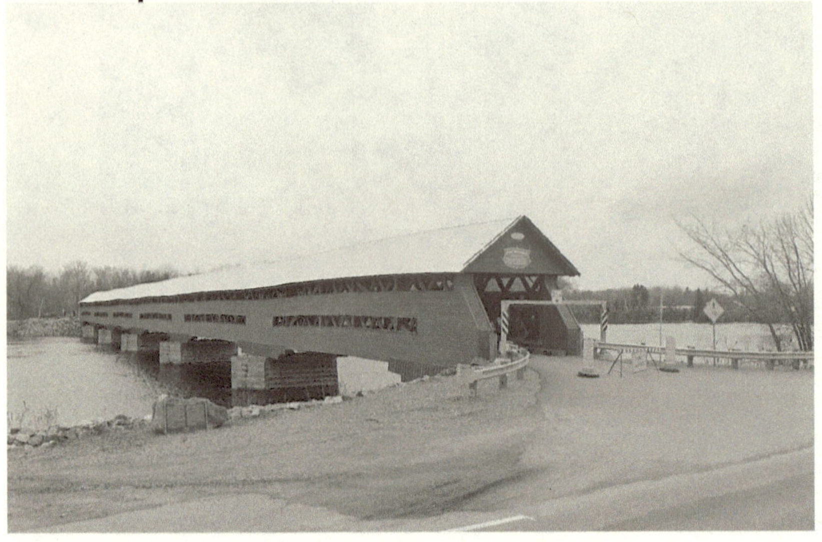

GPS Position: 45°51'41.0"N 76°44'26.0"W
Directions: From Mansfield-et-Pontefract, head northwest on QC-148 O for 1.2 km and turn left onto Chem. du Pont Rouge and the bridge
Crosses: Rivière Coulonge
Carries: Chem. du Pont Rouge
Builder: Augustus Brown
Year Built: 1898 (R12964) (R1997) (R2021)
Truss Type: Town and Queen
Dimensions: 6 Spans, 152 meters, 499 feet
Notes: This is the longest covered bridge in the province. It was named for Félix-Gabriel Marchand, prime minister of Québec. It was restored in 1964, 1997 and 2021.

World Index Number: QC/61-53-01
Formerly Listed in County: Pontiac

Pont du Faubourg
Region: Saguenay-Lac-Saint-Jean
Township: Saint-Jean

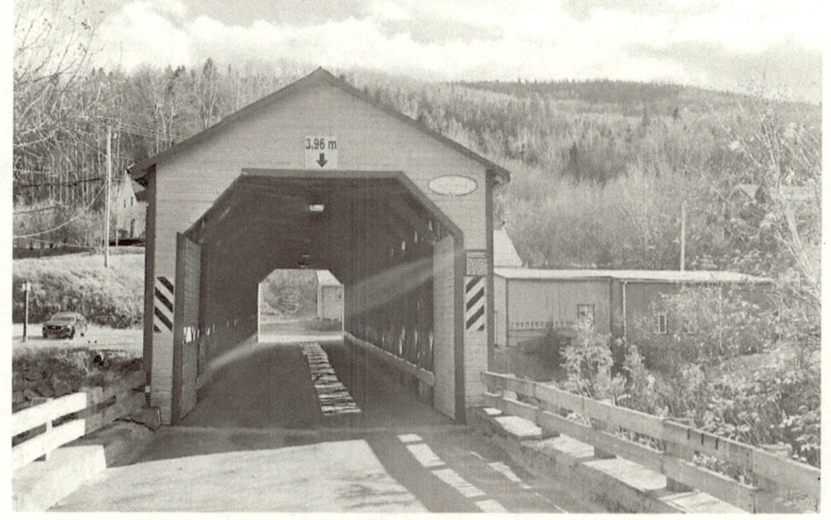

GPS Position: 48°14'05.0"N 70°12'10.0"W
Directions: From Les Trois-Ponts, head north on Rue Saint-Jean-Baptiste for 2.7 km and turn left onto Rue du Faubourg where the bridge is 250 m
Crosses: Rivière Saint-Jean
Carries: Rue du Faubourg
Builder: Not known
Year Built: 1929 (R1986)
Truss Type: Town variation
Dimensions: 1+ Span, 37 meters, 122 feet
Notes: The 1986 repairs were needed when the bridge was carried away by an ice jam. After repairs, it was returned to its site by transport truck. The central pier is a later addition.

World Index Number: QC/61-17-01
Formerly Listed in County: Chicoutimi

Pont du Lac-Ha! Ha!
Region: Saguenay-Lac-Saint-Jean
Township: Boilleau

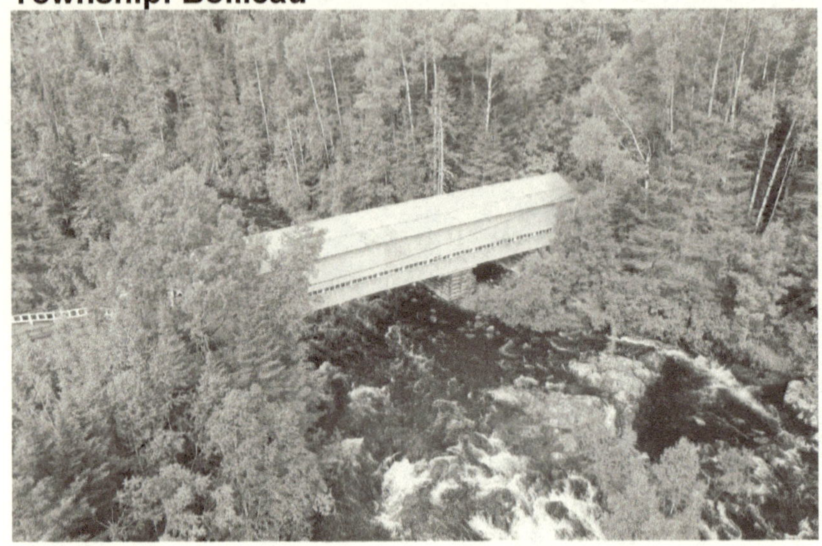

GPS Position: 48°04'00.0"N 70°49'27.0"W
Directions: From Boilleau, head south on QC-381 S for 2.2 km and turn right onto Chem. du Pont Couvert/Rte Ancienne 381 and find the bridge
Crosses: Rivière Ha! Ha!
Carries: Chem. du Pont Couvert/Rte Ancienne 381
Builder: Not known
Year Built: 1934
Truss Type: Town variation
Dimensions: 2 Spans, 37 meters, 122 feet
Notes: This bridge has been closed since the summer of 2010. It is the only covered bridge in Quebec whose panels are corrugated sheet metal. The bridge is currently green with white mouldings. It was formerly white with red mouldings
World Index Number: QC/61-17-04
Formerly Listed in County: Chicoutimi

Pont Rouge (Sainte-Jeanne d'Arc)

Region: Saguenay-Lac-Saint-Jean
Township: Dolbeau

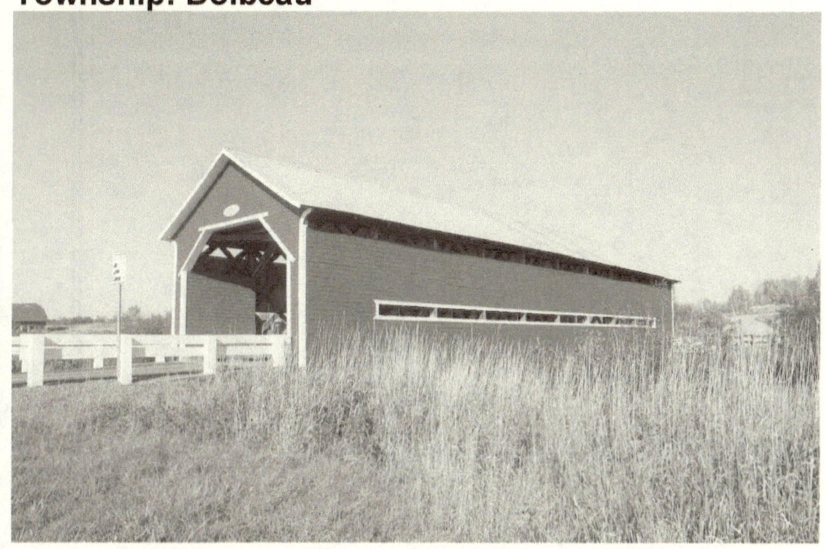

GPS Position: 48°52'59.0"N 72°05'05.0"W
Directions: From Sainte-Jeanne-d'Arc, head NW on Chem. Principal for 1.6 km and turn left onto Rte du Pont Couvert. After 1.1 km turn left onto Chem. du Pont Couvert and see the bridge
Crosses: Rivière Noire
Carries: Chem. du Pont Couvert
Builder: Not known
Year Built: 1936 (R1995) (R2013)
Truss Type: Town variation
Dimensions: 1 Span, 25 meters, 82 feet
Notes: Major repairs were needed in 1995 due to damage from an arson attack. An extensive rehabilitation was done in 2013. It is closed in winter.
World Index Number: QC/61-60-04
Formerly Listed in County: Roberval

Abiti-Est County Tour

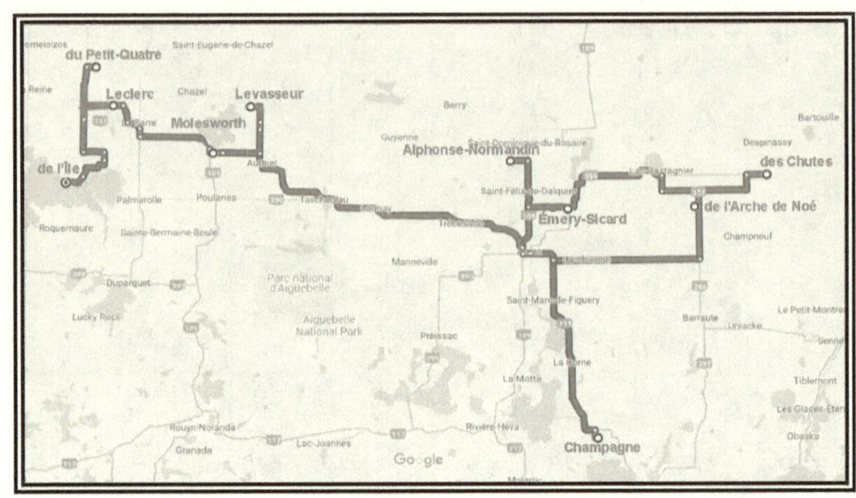

10 Bridges with 5 hours 20 minutes driving

Pont Champagne (Vassan) 48°12'53.0"N 77°55'32.0"W
Pont Alphonse-Normandin 48°44'04.0"N 78°09'49.0"W
Pont Émery-Sicard 48°38'36.0"N 78°00'18.0"W
Pont des Chutes 48°42'17.0"N 77°26'41.0"W
Pont de l'Arche de Noé 48°38'46.0"N 77°39'03.0"W
Pont Levasseur 48°50'07.0"N 78°53'22.0"W
Pont Molesworth 48°44'56.0"N 78°59'39.0"W
Pont Leclerc 48°50'11.0"N 79°16'33.0"W
Pont du Petit-Quatre 48°54'29.0"N 79°19'35.0"W
Pont de l'Île 48°41'30.0"N 79°24'27.0"W

Abiti-Ouest County Tour

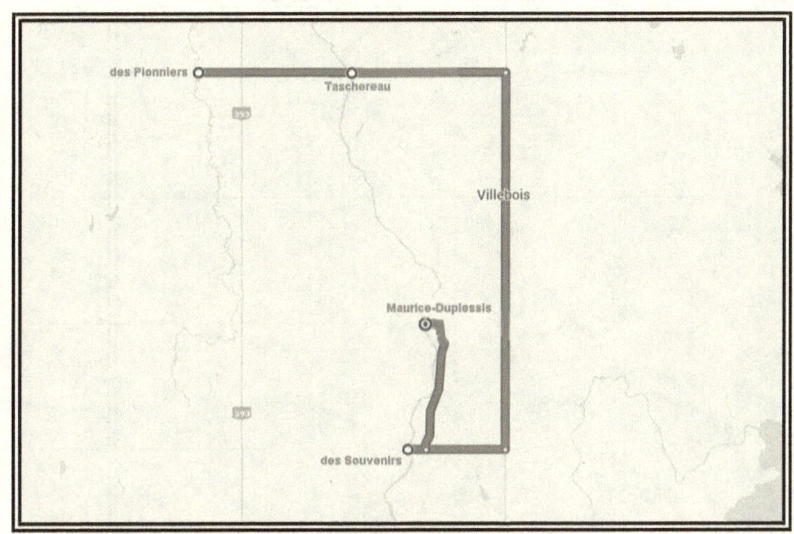

4 Bridges and 30 minutes driving

Pont des Pionniers	49°07'35.8"N 79°15'16.6"W
Pont Taschereau	49°07'35.0"N 79°12'03.0"W
Pont des Souvenirs	49°02'18.9"N 79°10'50.9"W
Pont Maurice-Duplessis	49°04'04.0"N 79°10'30.0"W

Compton County Tour

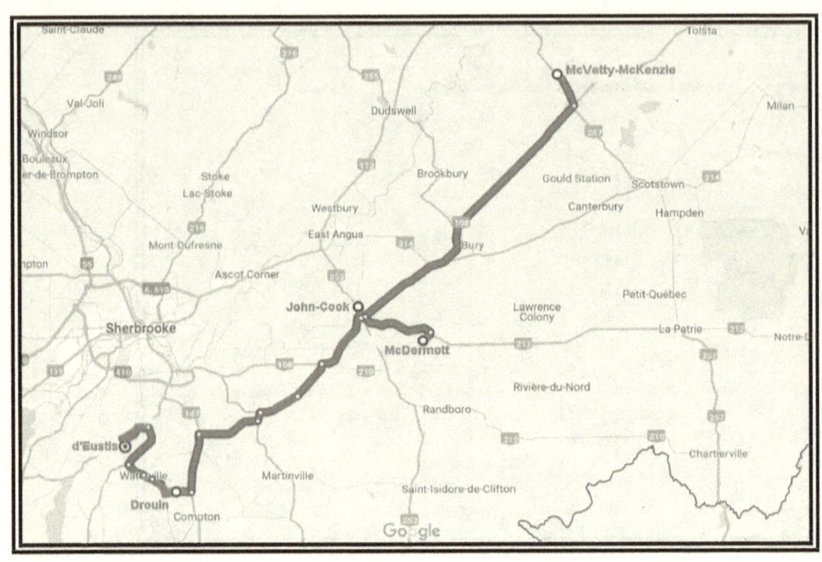

5 Bridges with 1 hour 15 minutes driving

McVetty-McKenzie	45°37'10.0"N 71°23'42.0"W
McDermott	45°23'34.0"N 71°33'22.0"W
John-Cook	45°25'19.0"N 71°37'57.0"W
Drouin	45°15'50.0"N 71°51'05.0"W
d'Eustis	45°18'11.0"N 71°54'48.0"W

Gatineau County Tour

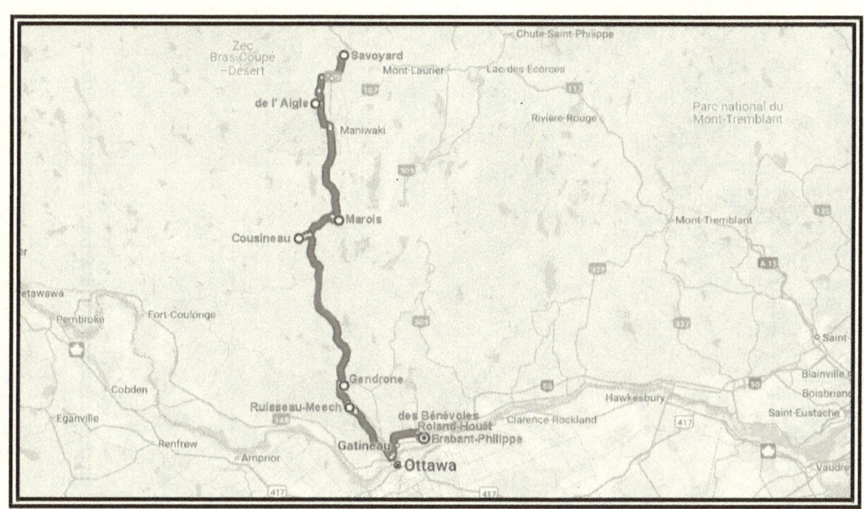

9 Bridges with 3 hours driving

Savoyard (Grand-Remous)	46°35'30.0"N 75°55'48.0"W
de l' Aigle	46°27'10.0"N 76°02'41.0"W
Marois	46°07'07.5"N 75°56'37.1"W
Cousineau	46°03'57.0"N 76°06'27.0"W
Gendrone (Wakefield)	45°38'44.6"N 75°55'06.2"W
Ruisseau-Meech	45°34'57.0"N 75°53'45.0"W
des Bénévoles	45°30'11.2"N 75°36'02.0"W
Roland-Houét	45°29'59.5"N 75°36'16.3"W
Brabant-Philippe	45°29'54.0"N 75°35'39.0"W

Labelle County Tour

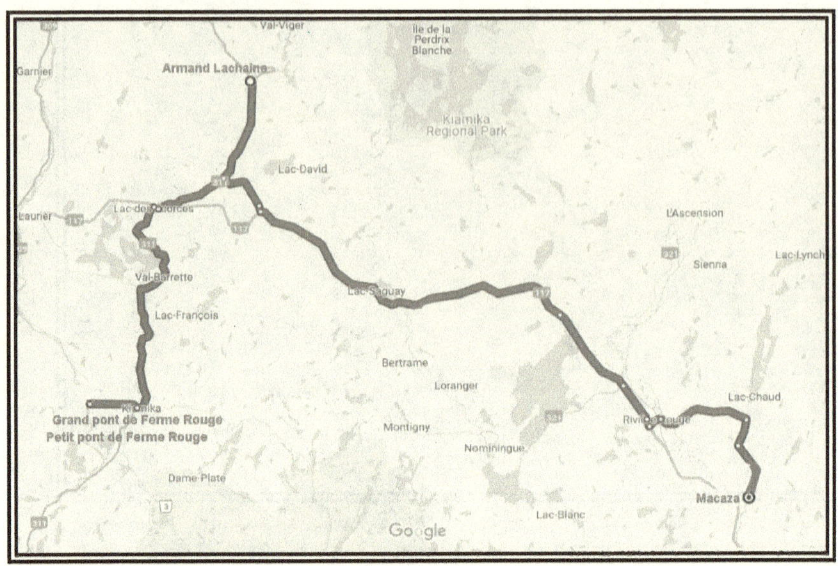

4 Bridges with 1 hour 30 minutes driving

Grand pont de Ferme Rouge	46°25'35.0"N 75°25'44.5"W
Petit pont de Ferme Rouge	46°25'35.1"N 75°25'40.0"W
Armand Lachaîne	46°38'36.0"N 75°16'08.0"W
Macaza	46°21'24.0"N 74°46'46.0"W

Matane County Tour

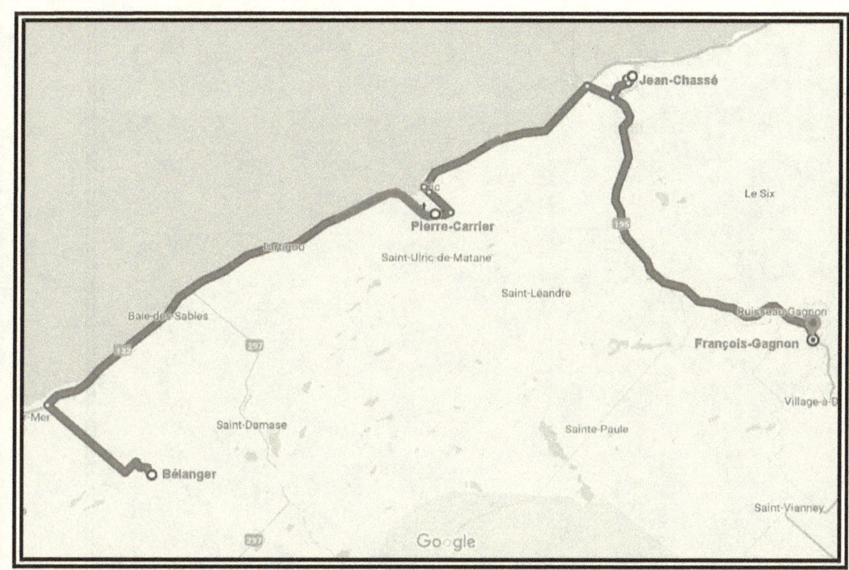

4 Bridges with 1 hour driving

Bélanger (Les Boules)	48°38'08.0"N 67°54'20.0"W
Pierre-Carrier	48°46'20.0"N 67°41'05.0"W
Jean-Chassé (St. Luc)	48°43'12.0"N 67°24'50.0"W
François-Gagnon	48°42'24.0"N 67°23'22.0"W

Matapédia County Tour

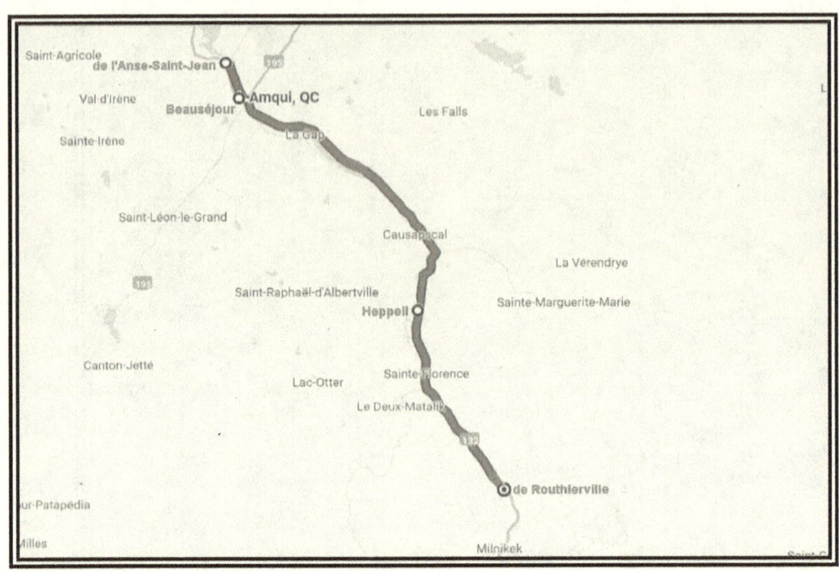

4 Bridges with 45 minutes driving

de l'Anse-Saint-Jean (Amqui)	48°29'31.0"N 67°26'54.0"W
Beauséjour	48°27'58.0"N 67°26'00.0"W
Heppell	48°18'43.0"N 67°14'29.0"W
de Routhierville	48°10'56.0"N 67°08'57.0"W

Glossary

Abutment: The abutments are the bridge supports on each side bank. Usually they were originally constructed of stone but they have often been replaced or supplemented with concrete through the years.

Arch: A curved timber or timber set which is shaped in a curve and functions as a support of the bridge.

Bed timbers: Timbers between the abutment and the truss or bottom chord.

Brace or bracing: A diagonal timber or timber set used to support the trusses.

Bridge Deck: The roadway through the bridge.

Buttress: Wood or metal members on the exterior sides which connect the floor beams and the top of the truss. Used to keep the bridge structure from twisting under wind, water and snow loads.

Camber: A planned curve in the structure to compensate for the weight of the structure.

Chord: The horizontal members extending the length of the truss meant to carry the load to the abutments.

Dead load: The load of the weight of the bridge itself.

Deck: The pathway through the bridge used by pedestrians or vehicles.

Pier: Stone/concrete supports built in the stream bed to support the bridge

Portal: The bridge's entrances.

Post: The truss's vertical members.

Span: The bridge length measured between the abutments.

Treenails or trunnels: Pins or dowels turned from hardwood, driven into holes drilled into the members of the truss to hold them together. Also used in mortised joints.

Truss: The framework which carries the load of the bridge and distributes it to the abutments.

Truss Types

A Truss is a system of ties and struts which are connected to act like a single beam to distribute and carry a load. In covered bridges, these Trusses carry the load to stone abutments at each side and perhaps piers in between.

Brown

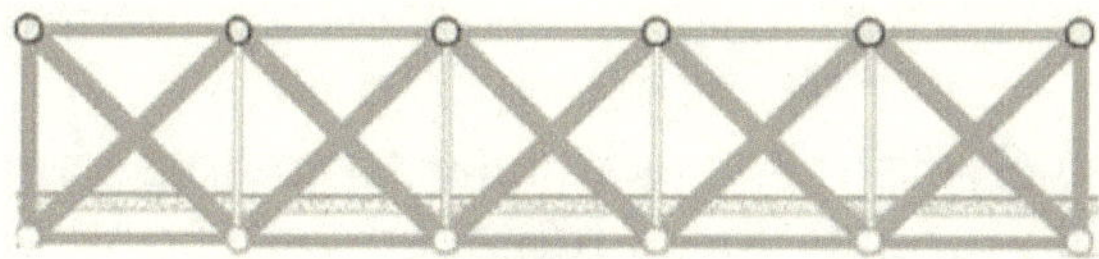

Brown

Josiah Brown Jr., of Buffalo, New York, patented this system in 1857.It consists of diagonal cross compression members connected to horizontal top and bottom stringers and is known for economic use of materials. It was only used in Michigan where there are a couple of surviving members.

Burr Arch

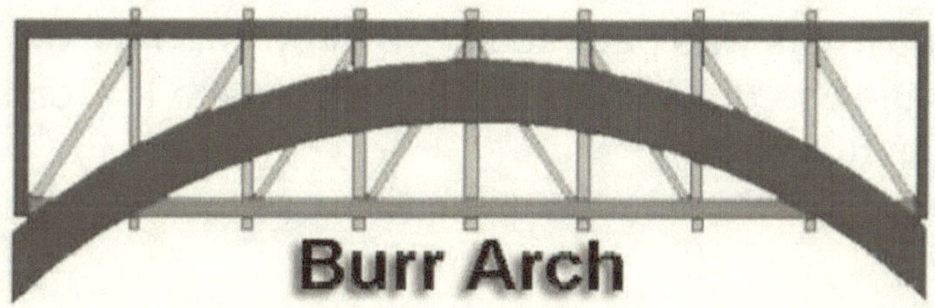

Burr Arch

Invented in 1804 by Theodore Burr, the Burr Arch is one of the most commonly found structures in Covered Bridge design. It is often used in combination with multiple kingposts. The ends of the arch are buried in the abutments

Childs

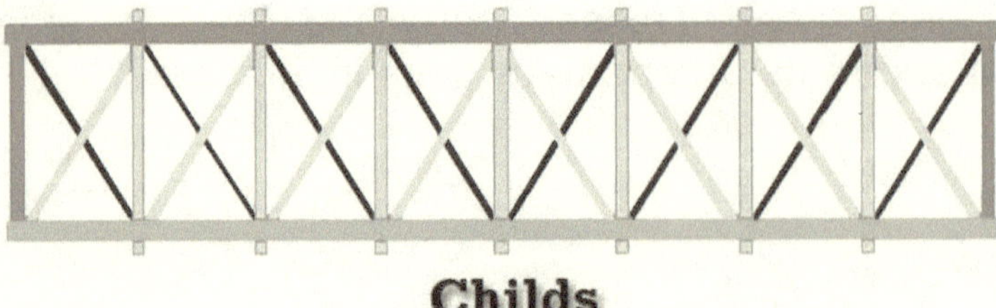

Childs

The Childs Truss System is essentially a multiple kingpost with half of the diagonal timbers replaced with iron bars.

Howe

Howe Truss

The Howe Truss was patented in 1840 by William Howe. It involves the use of vertical metal rods between the joints of wooden diagonals.

Kingpost

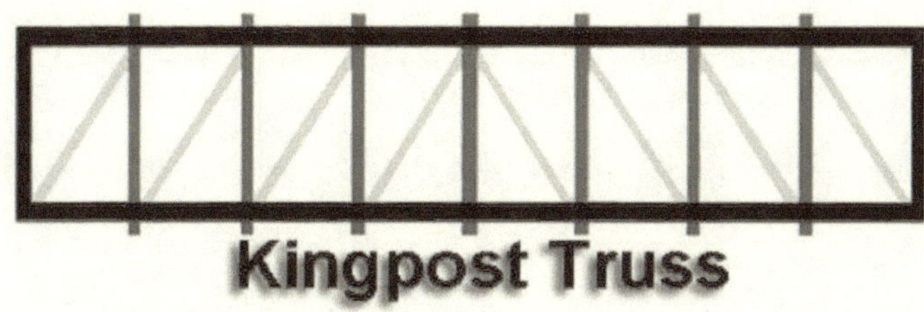

Kingpost is the simplest form of Truss with two diagonal members on a bottom chord, often with a vertical post connecting to the diagonals. The multiple Kingpost involves a series of Kingposts symmetrical from the bridges center. This allows for a much longer span.

Long

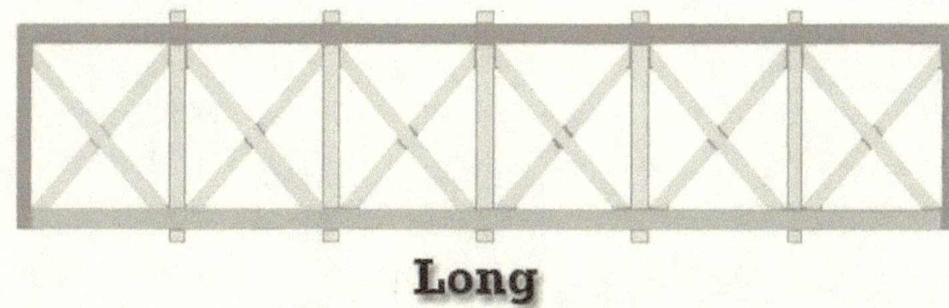

The Long Truss was patented by Stephen Long in 1830. It is a series of X shaped diagonals connected to vertical posts

Paddleford

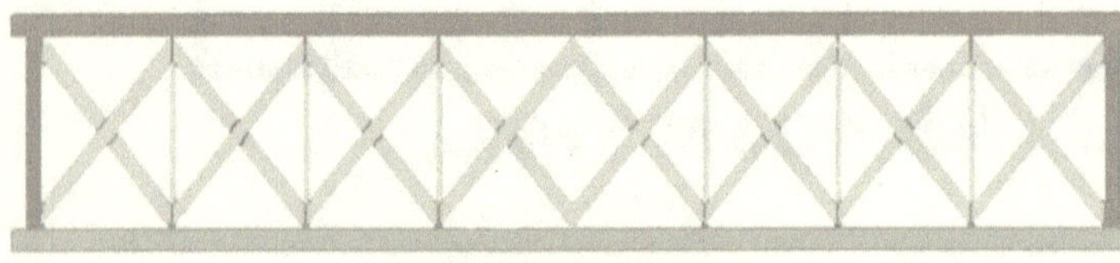

Paddleford

Peter Paddleford worked with the Long Truss system and eventually adapted it with a system of interlocking braces. he was never able to patent the system due to challenges from the owners of the Long Truss patent. However there are a number of New Hampshire and Vermont bridges which use the Paddleford system

Partridge

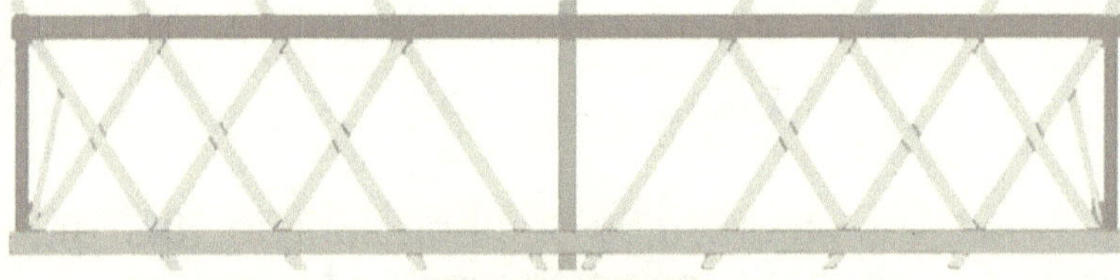

Partridge

Reuben L. Partridge received a patent for a design similar to the Smith system but adding terminal braces at the end and a central vertical member.

Pratt

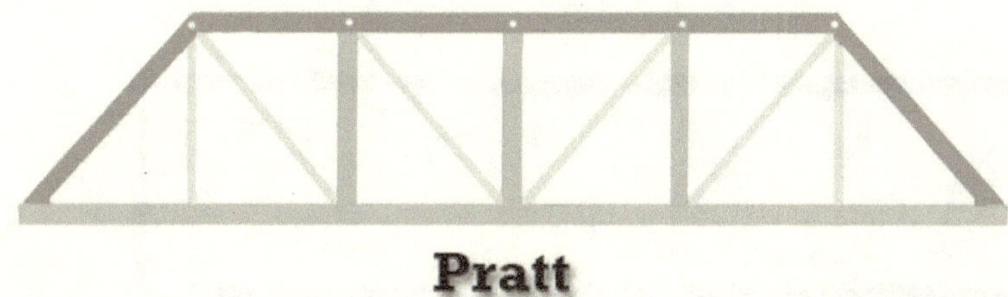

Pratt

The Pratt truss was patented in 1844 by Caleb Pratt and his son Thomas Willis Pratt. The design uses vertical members for compression and horizontal members to respond to tension.

Queenpost

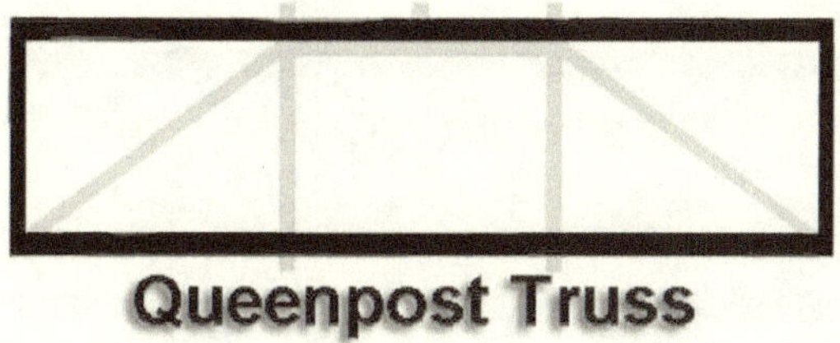

Queenpost Truss

The Queenpost has the peak of the kingpost type replaced with a horizontal top chord which allows for a longer span.

Smith

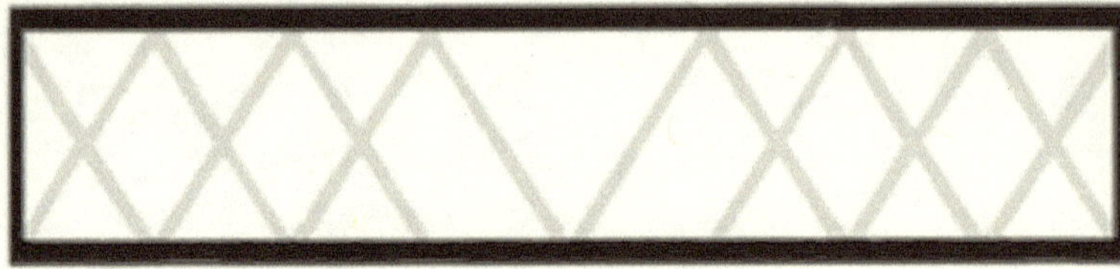

Smith Truss

Robert W. Smith received patents in 1867 and 1869 for variations of his system.

Town

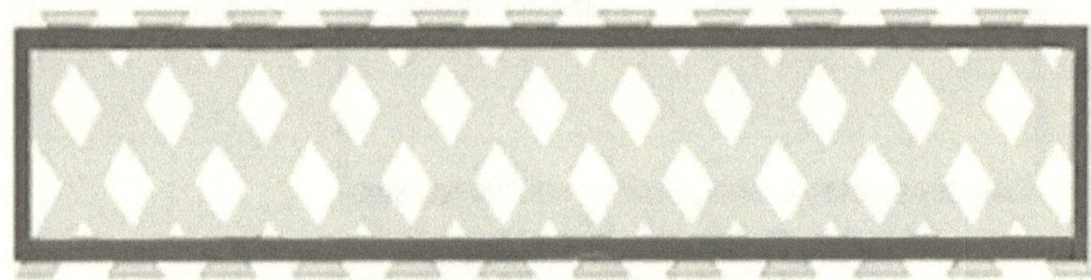

Town Truss

The Town or lattice system was patented by Ithiel Town in 1820. It involved a system of overlapping diagonals in a lattice pattern connected at the intersection by Tree nails or trunnels, wooden pegs or dowels. It had the advantages in that it could be constructed by unskilled labor and local materials could be used.

Warren

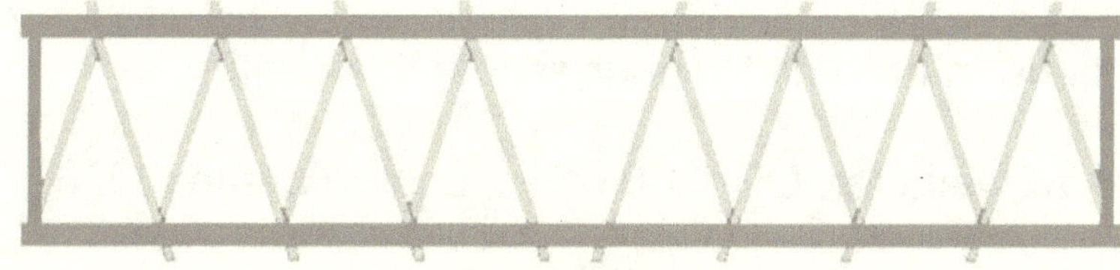

Warren

Patented in 1848 by two Englishmen, one of whom was named James Warren, it consists of parallel upper and lower chords with diagonal connecting members forming a series of equilateral triangles.

Recently Lost

Quebec has been hard hit for bridges lost this century

Saint-Félix-de-Dalquier, QC/61-01-21x, Lost to arson, 2006

Carrier, QC/61-01-28x, Burned 18 Aug 2011

du Canton Laas, QC/61-01-30x, Collapsed 2011

Davy or Chemin Hamel, QC/61-01-U01x, Arson 23 Sep 2020

de La Calamité, QC/61-02-04x, Lost to arson May 31, 2021

Blanc, QC/61-02-P01x, Burned 2019

de la Traverse, QC/61-02-P11x, Flood 2012

Kelly, QC/61-25-13x, Lost to Arson January 19, 2019

Coulée-Carrier, QC/61-42-03x, Flood 17 Nov 2007

Gareau, QC/61-46-01x, Collapsed Sep 2011

de Capelton, QC/61-67-02x, Lost to Arson, 19 Sept 2002

References

National Society for the Preservation of Covered Bridges
http://www.coveredbridgesociety.org

New York State Covered Bridge Society
http://www.nycoveredbridges.org

Vermont Covered Bridge Society
http://www.vermontbridges.com/

Covered Bridge Society of Oregon
http://www.covered-bridges.org/

The Theodore Burr Covered Bridge Society of Pennsylvania
http://www.tbcbspa.com/

Indiana Covered Bridge Society
http://www.indianacrossings.org/

Ohio Historic Bridge Association
http://oldohiobridges.com/ohba/index.htm

Harold Stiver Image Gallery
https://haroldstiver.smugmug.com/Galleries/Themes/Covered-Bridges

Photo Credits:

Amqui, Jean-Chassé, François-Gagnon; **Csapbat**, La Macaza; **Fralambert**, Bordeleau, de Saint-Mathieu, de Saint-Edgar, Heppell, Romain-Caron, Taschereau; **Guerinf**, Armand, Champagne; **JeffT**, Rouge; **Johny-le-cowboy**, ste-jeanne-darc; **Khayman**, Belanger; **Pascal721,** Denommee, Bolduc, Landry, Levasseur, de l'Arche-de-Noé; **Michel Rathwell**, Beauséjour; **R. L'Heureux**, Saint-Andre; **RaynaultM**, de Wakefield; **Yanick Pelletierm**, des Défricheurs, du Sault; **Ymblanter**, Pierre-Carrier

All other Images are by the author

The Photographer's and Explorer's Series

Unless noted, there are Print and eBook editions available for the following.

Birding Guide to Orkney
Guide to Photographing Birds

Maine Lighthouses
Ontario Lighthouses

Ontario's Old Mills

Ontario Waterfalls

Alabama Covered Bridges (eBook)
California Covered Bridges (eBook)
Connecticut Covered Bridges (eBook)
Georgia Covered Bridges (eBook)
Indiana Covered Bridges
Maine Covered Bridges (eBook)
Massachusetts Covered Bridges (eBook)
Michigan Covered Bridges (eBook)
New Brunswick Covered Bridges
New England Covered Bridges
Covered Bridges of the Mid-Atlantic
Quebec Covered Bridges
Covered Bridges of the South
Missouri Covered Bridges
New Hampshire Covered Bridges
New York Covered Bridges
Ohio's Covered Bridges
Oregon Covered Bridges
The Covered Bridges of Kentucky (eBook)

The Covered Bridges of Kentucky and Tennessee
The Covered Bridges of Tennessee (eBook)
Vermont's Covered Bridges
The Covered Bridges of Virginia (eBook)
The Covered Bridges of Virginia and West Virginia
Washington Covered Bridges (eBook)
The Covered Bridges of West Virginia (eBook)
West Coast Covered Bridges

Index

www.ingramcontent.com/pod-product-compliance
Lightning Source LLC
LaVergne TN
LVHW091006080826
845145LV00003B/1154

* 9 7 8 1 9 2 7 8 3 5 3 9 5 *